Contents

© The Basic Skills Agency, Commonwealth House, 1-19 New Oxford Street, London, WC1A 1NU.

ISBN 1 85990 089 5

Design: Studio 21

First edition published January 1993

Revised March 1999

Reprinted May 2002

1 | Some Aspects of Adult Literacy

> The scale of the literacy problem – The definition of basic skills – The good reader – The good writer – How people learn – Experiences of learning – Diversity – Some styles of provision (Group work, 1:1 tuition, Open learning, Learning support, Individual IT, Distance learning)

This chapter looks at what literacy involves and why it is important. It examines the previous experiences of learning that students may bring and describes a range of styles of provision.

The scale of the literacy problem

Many chances and opportunities in life are denied to us if we are not literate enough to do the things we want to do. Both at work and as a member of society, it is difficult to take advantage of opportunities if we doubt our ability to cope with the communication skills this may involve. Perhaps the best way to illustrate this is to think of all the times in the day we read or write something and imagine what effect it would have on our life if we couldn't read or write very well.

The United Kingdom was one of the first industrialised countries to recognise that there were a large number of adults in need of improved literacy skills. Before 1975, literacy provision was on a small scale, often provided by small voluntary organisations offering individual tuition using volunteer tutors in students' homes.

Since then, there has been a significant increase in the scale of adult literacy provision. In England and Wales in the 1970s fewer than 15,000 people were receiving help with reading and writing. By the academic year 1994-95, this had risen to over 97,000 and there was a further 16% increase to 113,000 by 1997.

The 1997 report *It Doesn't Get Any Better* based on the National Child Development Study revealed that compared to those with adequate skills, adults with poor basic skills are:

- up to 5 times more likely to be unemployed or out of the labour market;
- more likely to live in a household where both partners are not in paid employment;
- more likely to have children at an earlier age, and to have more children;

- more likely to have children who also struggle with basic skills;
- less likely to own their own home;
- less likely to be in good health;
- less likely to be involved in public life, a community organisation or to vote;
- more likely to be homeless;
- over-represented in prisons and young offenders institutions.

Good reading, writing, speaking and listening skills are not only important in our everyday and social lives, but also in the workplace. In the survey practical difficulties with literacy were most frequently mentioned in relation to work. 44% could not read a simple fire notice and 26% had problems filling in work related forms.

Basic skills is not just a simple matter of whether someone can read, write or calculate. Rather it's about how people cope with everyday tasks in a complex, industrialised society. So, for example, while only 5% of the survey could not understand part of a very simple advertisement, 18% could not understand what to do if you want more information about a career advertisement through a more complex advert.

We know that the need for help with basic skills continues to be considerable. In the early 1990s it was estimated that almost six million adults in the UK had some difficulty with basic skills including numeracy (1 in 6 of the population). In 1996 an international study of literacy standards in industrialised countries carried out by the Office of National Statistics (ONS) indicated that the number may be nearer 1 in 5, and showed Britain as having more people at the lowest level of competence than many comparable countries.

The 1997 report from the Social Statistics Research Unit at City University based on the NCDS group born in 1958 and surveyed at the age of 38 painted a depressing picture.

'As they reach "the heart of adult life" it's clear that problems with basic skills have a continuing, adverse effect on their lives. People with limited basic skills are less likely than those with good basic skills to have a job. Critically, the research shows a widening gap. As jobs require more skills, those with limited skills are increasingly marginalised. They are less likely to have been promoted or to have had training at work. They are less likely to be a member of a public organisation or to vote in a general election. The evidence of this report gives a stark picture of disadvantage in the labour market and social exclusion.'

(It Doesn't Get Any Better published by Basic Skills Agency, 1997)

The definition of basic skills

When we talk about basic skills we mean:

'The ability to read, write and speak in English and use mathematics at a level necessary to function and progress at work and in society in general'.

In Wales basic skills includes the ability to read and write Welsh for adults whose mother tongue is Welsh.

Our definition of basic skills does not include necessarily wider provision for adults with learning difficulties or other special needs, English as a Foreign Language (EFL) or general access and return to study courses. A range of 'key skills' has been identified which are often relevant to vocational training. The term 'basic skills' is related to, and is fundamental in, two of these: Communication and Application of Number, but does not cover Problem Solving, Information Technology or Working with Others.

The good reader

For a fluent reader many things become automatic and they may not appreciate the complicated range of skills they use. Logging the activities of a single day highlights the extent and variety of typical reading materials:

- letters and circulars;
- newspapers;
- street signs and billboards;
- checking a diary for appointments;
- following a recipe;
- looking up a phone number;
- reading a novel;
- looking up the times of TV programmes.

Most adults who are new to reading expect it to be one activity – a careful and accurate translation of written remarks into sound and meaning.

A good reader moves easily in and out of reading styles – sometimes speedily looking through to pick out the main points, sometimes searching a text for a particular bit of information and ignoring the rest, sometimes studying the whole piece in great detail. A good reader is able to break down the 'code' of print, by converting letter shapes into sounds and then words, we call this **'de-coding'**.

The good reader reads for a purpose:

- to perform the tasks demanded by a job i.e. follow instructions on using the photocopier;
- to help reach decisions in one's personal life i.e. which holiday company offers the better deal;
- to catch up with news from a friend abroad when an airmail letter arrives;
- to grasp an outline of something before deciding whether to continue reading.

Points to notice

1. Reading does not need to be performed aloud – in very few situations do adults read out loud.
2. Different reading approaches need to be taught and practised – they don't just happen.
3. Focusing on the purpose of the reading will help students see the sense of this.

The good writer

Good writers are able to adapt their writing skills for a number of everyday purposes:
- a letter to a friend;
- birthday and Christmas cards;
- a sick note to your child's teacher;
- a letter of complaint;
- filling in a detailed form for insurance;
- a tax return;
- accident reports at work;
- essays for college courses;
- making a note of what has been recorded on a video.

Good writers are able to try different ways of putting words together until they feel happy with what they have written. They are willing to have a go, realising that most people need to do things in "rough", make changes and then polish it up. The tutor may describe such stages as **"first draft"**, **"editing"**, and **"final copy"**.

Many students find writing a demanding and complex activity – so much to remember and do at the same time. Teaching approaches which break this down into separate stages take some of the pressure off the students.

As experience grows the good writer learns to distinguish between two families of skills.

1. Composition – considering the content:

- what thoughts they wish to get across;
- judging what order to put them in;
- deciding on how to start and finish well and linking the main points together;
- choosing words that accurately express meaning.

2. Transcription – the secretarial side of writing:

- making decisions about the layout and presentation (e.g. writing the final copy of a letter on a writing pad rather than lined exercise paper; deciding whether to word process a piece or present it in handwriting);

- making sure that the words used are spelt correctly (NB: this is not the same as using only the words you can spell - a ploy of many anxious student writers);

- checking that the grammar and punctuation are as suited to the purpose of the writing (e.g. It is appropriate to be formal in a letter to the Housing Department at the Town Hall, but more informal and relaxed when writing an article for a student magazine);

- re-reading the piece carefully to make sure that it really says what the writer thinks it does (small words have a habit of getting missed out when the writer's ideas flow faster than his pen).

The tutor may use the term **'proof reading'** for these various checks under **Transcription**.

How people learn

A major problem for many tutors is distinguishing between teaching and learning. Unfortunately just because the tutor is teaching it does not mean that the student is learning. Learning can only be accomplished by the student, the tutor's task is to facilitate the process.

> *"I hear and I forget,*
> *I see and I remember,*
> *I do and I understand."*

This is a well known old Chinese proverb which all tutors should heed. All learning is best done through active involvement. Imagine you are learning to use a new computer, you could listen to a tutor telling you how to use it, you could watch somebody using a computer or you could practise on a computer with the assistance of the tutor when you required it. It is likely that the latter method, whereby you get **"hands on"** experience would be the best.

The most effective way of learning is by doing. For successful learning to take place it is essential that:

- the skills to be learned are relevant to the student and student's needs;
- students can learn to use these skills in different contexts and activities;
- the student is actively involved in the process;
- the student is allowed to work at their own pace.

It is important to remember that students start at different points, have different goals/ needs and work at different speeds. The best learning programmes are designed to build on strengths and minimise the areas of weakness that the student brings.

Common problems in all teaching are:

- how to motivate;
- how to sustain interest.

It is of utmost importance to put the student first. Remember that adult students are not a homogeneous group and they respond differently to different learning situations. Beginner readers usually need plenty of reassurance and support whereas the student who is a confident reader will require some independence and autonomy in the learning process.

It is equally important to keep sight of your role as tutor. The end result of basic skills tuition should be that a student has improved literacy skills and can use them independently. Your job is to make yourself redundant to the student as quickly as possible. Therefore the emphasis of your work should be to allow the student to demonstrate newly learnt literacy skills. An effective student-tutor relationship is one where the student shines, rather than the tutor.

Experiences of learning

When students have very little confidence in their ability to learn, it can be useful to spend some time talking about the successful learning they have experienced. A list of these experiences, both in and out of school, might cover a wide range and include such things as:

- learning job routines and processes at work;
- learning about bringing up children and dealing with their problems;
- learning to drive;
- remembering addresses and telephone numbers;
- learning other school subjects, perhaps practical ones like woodwork or needlework;
- learning to do household jobs.

It may also be useful to look at other experiences which have not been successful, particularly as we often learn from failing at a task and students need to be aware that this is a part of all learning. Unwillingness to try, and risk failure, is often negative and means we only attempt learning things we feel sure of succeeding in.

You may find it useful to think of one or two of your own learning experiences which did not prove successful. The idea is to try and pinpoint what were the main reasons for failure. The list you come up with is likely to include:

- low opinion of your own ability;

- lack of confidence;

- lack of stimulation, leading to boredom;

- stress;

- poor relationship with teacher;

- change of teacher;

- lack of appropriate teaching;

- no support from others;

- distraction in the teaching environment;

- too much use of jargon;

- competitive atmosphere;

- too much information at once;

- poor memory.

By talking about these factors you can begin to see how learning is affected by many things other than intelligence. It is also a relief for the student to find that other people have failed for similar reasons.

As one tutor said:

'I've just realised why I never play darts. It's the scoring that I'm scared of. My friends have been playing for years and have no trouble adding up the scores really quickly. I guess I just don't want to show myself up.'

There will be times when no new learning seems to be taking place – when a student appears to have reached a plateau and cannot move forward. This is quite usual, and probably means that the student needs to review and practise what has gone before, to consolidate learning. It may mean a re-assessment of the materials and teaching methods used or a complete revision of the learning plan.

If a student has specific learning difficulties (often termed 'dyslexia'), they will need specialist help and support. They may have particular problems with memory, auditory or perceptual difficulties, which may require more specialised approaches. Such help is often available through specially trained staff. There are references to sources of help at the end of this book.

Diversity

There are now greater opportunities for adults to learn, and a growing number of contexts where they can learn. Often these contexts come about, so that adults can learn what they want, where they can.

Currently there are six major basic skills programmes:

- discrete basic skills courses in colleges, adult centres and voluntary organisations;
- support for students on other courses;
- vision for unemployed;
- workplace programmes;
- family literacy courses;
- community-based programmes.

Some styles of provision

Much adult literacy provision was based on individual teaching, alternative styles of tuition have since developed.

- **Group work**
- **1:1 tuition**
- **Open learning**
- **Basic skills support and vocationally and occupationally linked teaching**
- **Individual IT**
- **Distance learning**

have become available in many areas.

Group work

Students coming along to improve their reading, writing and spelling may feel nervous initially. Through they know that other people in the room are also learning, they may suspect that everyone else is better than they are. In consequence they are keen to discuss their work only with the tutor. However, regular time for working in a group can provide benefits that the tutor alone cannot.

There are positive advantages in being part of a group. Low self esteem is often a barrier to learning. In a group, students can feel that they are part of a "student body". This enables them to see themselves not as isolated individuals, embarrassed by their lack of basic skills, but as adults entitled to the full range of educational opportunities. Members of a group can work together and help each other by pooling ideas, skills and knowledge. Material based on one theme can be produced at different levels so that students working at, say, Entry Level and those at Levels 1 or 2 can contribute and learn equally. Any individual difficulties can be covered in follow up work.

1:1 tuition

Working as a tutor with a student on a one to one basis may happen in basic skills classes or through open learning in a college. There may also be an occasional need for this type of tuition when trying to accommodate people confined to their homes or those who have irregular working patterns. One to one tuition is not normally a permanent arrangement and happens usually when a student is new to provision and needs considerable support until some degree of independence is achieved, or for a student who needs some intensive work on a specific personal need e.g. an imminent driving test. This support is often provided by a trained volunteer. The volunteer will be guided and supported by the tutor. As in other types of provision, students would determine their own style of working, setting their own pace and establishing their own goals.

Open learning

Open learning centres use a variety of learning methods which differ according to the individual student's needs. The range of learning opportunities include:

- timetabled individual tutorials;
- self access to resource based learning;
- independent study with tutorial support;
- distance learning;
- short courses;
- supplementary access to resources for existing basic skills students;
- discussion groups.

The concept of using computers in the delivery of basic skills to help students move towards their learning goals is fundamental to open learning. The use of technology, particularly the integration of information technology (IT) into basic skills work has been for many students their first opportunity to develop IT skills. The availability of good quality resources and equipment is a strong attraction in open learning and attracts many adults who would not attend traditional classes. Overall open learning centres have made a significant impact on provision and in many areas have helped to promote a high profile basic skills service. Well resourced basic skills centres, open for a large number of hours per week and in many cases throughout the year, have changed attitudes to post school education. The effectiveness and success of open learning provision depends upon:

- the flexibility of opening times;
- the availability of material that students can use independently;
- good record keeping and administration procedures.

Learning support

However it is organised, basic skills provision always seeks to put the students' needs first. For someone on a vocational course who is experiencing basic skills difficulties, the priority may simply be to keep up with the course content. Many colleges and training organisations provide basic skills learning support to students on mainstream courses. Through a learning support unit – basic skills specialists organise sessions outside the course timetable for those who are struggling with the essential reading, writing or basic maths demanded by their vocational course. Organisation of work, and study skills are also offered. As in other basic skills provision, the student has a confidential interview with the learning support tutor, individual strengths and weaknesses are looked at in the context of the mainstream course. The outcome is an individual learning plan discussed and agreed by student and tutor which sets realistic goals for the short and longer term. Basic skills support is normally offered in an informal workshop setting. Students may book a regular time or just drop in, and they are encouraged to work as independently as possible. The workshops provide wide ranging materials, computer facilities and other technological aids. In some cases learning support is offered in other ways. Sometimes a basic skills tutor is timetabled into a course to work alongside a vocational lecturer – double staffing certain sessions.

On some vocational courses basic English and maths are integrated into the course content so that all students are targeted for help. In addition most supervisors in Youth and Adult Training Schemes also integrate basic English and maths work into their workshop practices.

Increasingly, vocational lecturers are taking up training opportunities to develop their awareness of basic skills approaches. This helps them increase their strategies for presenting information clearly and simply, and probably benefits **all** their students.

Individual IT

The development of windows based programmes which can be navigated by the use of visual icons without screens full of text instructions has helped many adult learners to gain confidence in the use of IT. Software on CD-Rom is available which can guide the user to and through the task without the need for a lot of tutor support. The pace is dictated by the student. This encourages a valuable attitude of independence. As well as building in explanations and examples, programmes may score and record the student's performance for later tutor follow up of errors and teaching points.

Distance learning

For some students attendance at a centre or college may not be feasible. They may live in an inaccessible rural location or have heavy family commitments caring for elderly relatives or a sick child. In many circumstances, distance learning may provide a way forward. The link tutor meets the learner at a suitable venue, possibly their home, to interview the student and gauge their needs. Together they discuss and agree some learning targets.

Suitable learning materials are then provided for home study and the student sends completed work to the tutor for assessment and feedback. Distance learning resources may include audio tapes and videos as well as paper based assignments and the tutor may be available on a helpline at pre-arranged times.

2 | Student Profiles

In this section we will look at four people, each at a different level of literacy. In each case the tutors have given some background information about the students and their reasons for entering provision. Throughout the rest of the book, reference is made to the case studies, highlighting points we think are important including a summary of the techniques the tutor was using and why. Finally we include some ideas on how the work could be developed. Some of the ideas are for individual work, others could be used with either groups or individuals. All of them could and should be adapted to meet the problems faced by the student.

Case Study 1: NORMA

'I always know what I want to say to people but I can't write it down.'

Norma is 60 years old, and recently widowed. Her three children have married and do not live close by. She has had a job as a lunchtime organiser at the local primary school for many years, and for the past five years has been a voluntary helper at a local old folks home.

Norma grew up as the eldest of a large family. Her mother suffered from recurrent ill health and consequently **Norma** had to shoulder much of the responsibility of looking after her younger brothers and sisters. This meant that she frequently missed school and never managed to catch up with her education.

Because of her lack of confidence in reading and writing, after they married, **Norma's** husband took over responsibility for anything involving these skills. When her husband became terminally ill, he made enquiries about local literacy help – he was determined that she would not be left to struggle without him. Following his death, **Norma** rang the local referral number for literacy help.

Norma is now settled in a class at her local library which she attends once a week. It is six months since she joined the group and **Norma** already feels more confident.

'It's been hard since my husband died, but I get so much support from my tutor. It's been such a help to have somewhere I could bring any letters or forms I've needed to deal with. I couldn't have managed without the group.'

Case Study 2: JOE

Joe is 51 and in full time work which means that he is able to attend a class for only a couple of hours a week. At school his one interest was football and as he himself says,

'When it came to reading and writing, I think at first it wouldn't sink in so after a while, the teachers gave up trying to teach me.'

Although he had always been an under confident reader, he hadn't felt motivated to improve his reading until the threat of redundancy forced him to consider the skills he would need in the present job market. He had also, after some hesitation, agreed to become the local shop steward and was experiencing difficulty in understanding some of the correspondence and minutes of meetings involved in this work.

Although he was prepared to 'have a go' at most of these things he was never very confident that he had fully understood what he had read. His style when reading was to concentrate on one word at a time with frequent long hesitations before unfamiliar words. He always tried to sound out these unknown words which proved to be a very unsuccessful strategy for him, as this would often result in him coming up with guesses which made no sense in the passage. Not surprisingly this meant that he ended up understanding very little of what he read.

Case Study 3: PATRICIA

Patricia is in her early thirties with a two year old child. She is unemployed, has slight mobility problems and is registered as disabled. Her disability meant that her full time education took place in a special school, although nowadays she would have attended a mainstream school.

Unfortunately her school experience did not help to develop her self confidence, and when she first attended classes she was painfully shy. From school she moved into an industrial training unit sponsored by a charity. The unit had some basic education facilities which **Patricia** attended. After assessment by the tutor there she was referred to a local adult education centre because it was felt that both her social and educational horizons could better be developed outside the unit.

Gaining qualifications was an important goal for her - she particularly wanted to achieve a GCSE in English.

"No-one ever took any exams at my school and nobody expected very much of any of us. I always felt I could achieve something if only I was given the chance."

Case Study 4: ANSELL

Ansell is an 18 year old British born black student on a catering course at a North West further education college. He explains,

'The practical work is the best part – that's really what it's all about – but the reading and writing did my head in at first. I was so busy trying to take everything down that I often missed half the main points.'

Ansell was the last of four children. His mother came to Britain from Jamaica in the early 1960s and **Ansell** was born and brought up in the North West of England. He didn't enjoy school but his mother put great store by qualifications. She wouldn't let him go out until he'd done his homework. He was quite pleased when he got GCSE passes in Art and Maths, though his grades were low.

After leaving school at 16 he drifted from one training scheme to another. His most successful placement was working in the kitchens of a large hotel which he enjoyed. The Careers Adviser suggested he might follow this up and **Ansell** was accepted on a scheme at the local further education college.

The course focused on the practical skills needed for different cooking processes and **Ansell** was keen to learn. However, in class he found taking notes difficult and tended to miss things out. Remembering the new catering words was a bit of a problem, especially as some of them were in French. Even when copying from the board it was hard for him to keep up. **Ansell** knew that later in the course he would have to take down orders over the phone and fill out order forms and he felt worried about managing this.

During the first term he found it hard going and even considered giving up. **Ansell's** catering lecturer noticed his problems and suggested he might benefit from attending the college's Basic Skills Unit for learning support. She explained to **Ansell** that he could have extra study time to work on his reading, writing, spelling and study skills. He was a bit put out and said he could read already but was persuaded when she said she could see he had the ability but just needed the skills to organise himself.

3 | Assessment and Evaluation

Assessment – Initial assessment – Devising a student 'Learning Plan' –
Assessing progress – Record keeping – Lesson plans – Evaluating your
teaching – The tutor/student relationship

This chapter examines the processes of assessing the student, both when joining
provision and in regularly reviewing progress. It describes the setting of a learning plan
and stresses the importance of keeping individual records.

It emphasises the usefulness of written lesson plans and discusses how tutors can
evaluate their own teaching.

Assessment

Assessment is a vital process in the learning programme and it should not be confused
with the initial interview, which is often conducted by someone other than the tutor.
The initial interview sets out to give individuals the chance to:

- find out about the different kinds of tuition available;
- identify wider needs and goals;
- get advice and guidance.

For basic skills students assessment should be:

- collaborative;
- purposeful;
- non-threatening;
- of benefit to both tutor and student.

Assessment should take place at frequent stages in the learning process and time must
be set aside for regular review sessions. These reviews enable the tutor and the student,
to collect and assess evidence that the agreed goals have been attained.

Initial assessment

The aim of initial assessment is to provide a clear picture of the student's aptitudes,
attitudes and motivation, so that a meaningful learning plan can be negotiated. It gives
both tutor and student a chance to identify what the student:

- wants to achieve as a result of basic skills tuition;
- can already do;
- needs specific help with.

It may also provide valuable information on the student's strengths and weaknesses. For example, a student with a stronger visual memory may remember words by seeing them, using flashcards or other techniques that make use of this strength. By the same token approaches that require good auditory skills, for example sounding words out, may not be as successful with this student.

From the initial assessment the tutor is able to build up a list of **competences** that the student already has, and others that go to make up the goals that he or she has. A good approach to this is to use the Basic Skills Standards. These apply to all basic skills work. So, for example, a student might work towards the following goals:

- **extract information and meaning from a variety of graphical sources;**

- **convey ideas feelings and experiences in writing;**

- **complete a form.**

In addition, the standards describe the skills that underpin most reading and writing. It is essential that students learn to use these skills. And your assessment should identify which of these skills students do or don't possess. So, for example, the skills of writing that are under the two standards above include:

- Unit 304, Element 2   • Unit 305, Element 3   • Unit 305, Element 3.

For many students the achievement of success in literacy, when it is recorded in these terms, can open up the chance to gain some kind of qualification (see *Part 5*).

Initial assessment should take place when a student first enters provision and can take a variety of forms:

- informal interview;
- analysis of pieces written by the student;
- set screening tests;
- computer based or multi-media exercises.

Ansell

Ansell's learning support tutor used a 'Cloze Test' to decide what level of reading matter he could easily understand. Cloze testing is an adult alternative to hearing somebody read aloud. Passages are chosen at various levels of difficulty and words are deleted on a systematic basis every fifth word. The 'test' is presented as a puzzle. Its completion depends on a number of skills involved in reading:

- recognising words;
- prediction;

- skimming to recap what has been said;
- scanning to search for information to help predict;
- looking for meaning outside the context of the sentence.

'Cloze' is a rough way of deciding a person's overall reading ability. **Ansell** could manage level 'b' very well, (see below). This is the level at which popular newspapers are usually pitched. Level 'c', (see page 22) was more difficult and close to the level of a course text book. It was evident that **Ansell** would need more practice at this level to cope with his course.

READING ASSESSMENT   Section B

Cooking for a living

◀ VERSION 1

Cooking as a job is not the same as cooking at home. You cook for far larger numbers and use different equipment. Sometimes you have to use different methods of cooking.

In fast food restaurants (1) __for__ take-aways the food is (2) __made__ as people order. The (3) __shop__ uses ready prepared food (4)__like__ as frozen pies, samosas (5) __and__ pizzas.

But working in (6) __a__ hotel or restaurant kitchen (7) __is__ very different. One person may (8) __be__ responsible for only (9) __some__ part of a meal. (10)__A__ example, you may prepare (11) __green__ vegetables or just make (12) __hot__ sauces.

A kitchen is (13) __a__ busy place and you (14) __our__ always on your feet. (15) __It__ is hot and tiring (16) __and__ often has unsocial hours. (17) __Working__ in a school or in (18) __an__ office canteen the hours will (19) __be__ more regular.

Training (20) __is__ usually on the job, but (21) __cooks__ can also do (22) __a__ variety of courses leading (23) __past__ a national qualification. You (24) __must__ do this part-time or (25) __on__ a full-time course.

Perhaps (26) __you__ could set up your (27) __catery__ business. Caterers are needed (28) __for__ parties and weddings. More (29) __and__ more pubs and wine (30) __bars__ are providing food so (31) __you__ might find work on (32) __a__ freelance basis.

Although it (33) __is__ hard work, there (34) __will be__ lots of opportunities. So, (35) __if__ you enjoy cooking, (36) __you__ might like cooking for a living.

Total:

21

36 Marks

Adapted and reproduced by kind permission of Lifetime Careers Wiltshire Ltd.

This is the end of the Reading Assessment.

from *Initial Assessment,* Basic Skills Agency

POTATOES

The ways of serving potatoes are numerous, but the real test of skill in potato cookery is the ability to cook them to perfection using simple methods.

For boiling, steaming, roasting or deep frying, _large_ potatoes are the most satisfactory; _but_ when shallow frying potatoes, _and_ making potato salad, new _potatoes_ will give a better _size_ . Younger potatoes are richer _with_ protein than the older _ones_ and are solid, waxy _and_ juicy in texture when cooked. As _some_ starch cells are immature in _all_ potatoes, they are not as easily digested as old _potatoes_ . The main nutrients found _in_ potatoes are: starch, water, _calcium_ C and cellulose.

Convenience potato products

As potatoes _are_ so versatile and easily _eaten_ , there are many convenience _junk_ products available:

Canned

- New potatoes _in_ salted water, ready for instant use.
- Potato salad in mayonnaise, _in_ for instant use.

Frozen

- Blanched: roast _frozen_ chipped potatoes that may _cooked_ deep fried or oven-baked _and_ frozen.
- Prepared: croquette _potatoes_ balls in batter, may be _fat_ fried or oven-baked from _frozen_ .

Dehydrated

- Instant potato flakes or _mash_ may be reconstituted with _hot_ water, butter and seasonings.

Packets crisps/sticks

- Various _crisps_ and shapes are available. _The_ packets are in 28g _bags_ for individual portions or _big_ packets for bulk uses. _The_ products have a short _shelf_ life of three months maximum. _Many_ are different varieties of _potatoes_ and they tend to _be_ suitable for different methods _of_ cooking.

For example, Majestic are suitable for frying, Epicure for boiling and baking. Some varieties, like King Edward, are suitable for any method.

(Taken from 'Food Preparation')

You will read to practice reading at
this level of difficulty. We will try some more passages later.

There are other methods of assessing students. For example, some FE colleges have developed screening and assessment tests for new students like **Ansell**. There are assessment models that relate specifically to competences. See the list of resources at the back of this book for further details.

Norma

For **Norma** it all began when she went along to her first session at the local library. She knew from her initial interview with the Referral Worker that the tutor would be expecting her. It had been agreed that she would arrive twenty minutes before the start of the session. She had already got a lot off her chest whilst chatting to the Referral Worker, so although nervous she wasn't too worried about the next step. They talked informally about **Norma's** past experiences – about herself, her family, her interests, job and school life and why she had decided to join a class. To get some idea of how **Norma** perceived her problem they went through a checklist together. This covered reading skills and writing skills and helped the tutor to identify some starting points. Next the tutor and **Norma** listed all the reading and writing tasks that she would find most difficult to manage on her own and which she needed to cope with fairly urgently.

The tutor suggested **Norma** try some writing to begin with. This gave the tutor a more accurate picture of **Norma's** difficulties and provided them with something to start work on. This was a difficult task for **Norma** although she gave it a try.

Devising a student 'Learning Plan'

The learning plan is the 'map' which will guide the student (and the tutor) as they work towards their goals. If it is done well, it can be the key to greater independence for the student – a means of taking greater control and responsibility for their own learning. For a learning plan to be effective it is essential that it is negotiated between the student and the tutor. It should:

- identify long and short term goals;
- contain an outline of the steps needed to achieve these goals;
- be written in clear, plain language;
- be reviewed regularly;
- be accessible to both the student and the tutor;
- lead to greater student autonomy;
- form a record of the work undertaken at each session.

Some examples of learning plans are shown overleaf.

Discussion/Reading/Writing

Name: Norma

Things I would like to work on during the next six weeks	Six weeks review: What can I do now? What needs practice?
Like to read books To write and send Christmas Cards Sort out bills	

Week ending	Main activities done this week	Comments, reminders for next week
1st Nov	Started language experience following discussion with Norma about her baking wedding cakes Began listing some family names	Tape Queen Street for Norma to take home and listen to Norma to bring in her correspondence which needs dealing with
8th Nov	Revised language experience Norma can sequence the lines and began individual word recognition Introduced the idea of putting together a file Began sections on family names, messages for cards and numbers for cheques * I wrote two letters for Norma to copy out, name and send off to Building Society and Mail Order Catalogue.	Taking words home to practise Taking name game of matching words and numbers

Student's name Ansell Lawrence

Date 16-10-98 Subject Basic Skills

Tutor A. Trainer Accreditation General Catering – Wordpower?

Student needs/aims: (What she/he wants to learn)

Referred by Catering Lecturer.
Needs general basic skills support including:

- note taking from lecturers
- remembering new catering vocabulary
- increased speed at copying
- organising study methods
- taking down phone messages
- spelling
- order forms

Student's long term aims:

Catering qualification – to work in a hotel

Target in six sessions:

Catering items – develop a checklist of words and meanings

Common abbreviations (to speed up note taking)

Work on organising his notes

Use word checklist for work on spelling methods

Assessing progress

Ongoing assessment is a regular review of the learning plan. It helps the student and the tutor to identify what progress has been achieved and which goals have been met. It provides an opportunity to evaluate the work done and set new targets where appropriate.

Many schemes have learning plans that have space where student and tutor assessment of progress can be recorded.

The main purpose of the review is a 'step back' a chance to look at:

Date	Topic	Where to find	Done
6-10-98	Cloze passages	Assessing Reading Pack	Level (b) okay (c) – too hard
27-10-98	Catering Checklist – match meanings to words	Catering Folder A	

Student Comments	Tutor Comments
(b) was easier because it was more like a story	A good attempt – we will do more practice later
A good way to learn the words	Mixing up Patissier with Poissonier in list of chefs

26

Review _____ Date _____

Were your targets achieved?

How did you know?

I can now:

I had most success with:

I need to improve on:

Next I would like to:

Student's signature _____ Tutor's signature _____

- the areas where progress has been made (things that the student can now do);
- the work that has not gone well (things that the student has not learnt);
- new areas of work that need to be tackled.

From this the next learning plan can be constructed. Ongoing assessment and evaluation gave **Patricia** an opportunity to think about her longer term goals as well as her immediate needs. Without this she may have continued in classes where she worked on functional writing tasks. On the surface such work would have helped with her spelling but would not have addressed her eventual aim to move on to a GCSE course.

Record keeping

It is important that the record keeping section of the learning plan is completed at each session particularly where the learning programme involves the student seeing a number of different tutors.

If comments are to be of any value they must be constructive. Statements like *'I did some writing'*, or *'It was OK'* don't adequately describe what went on in the session. It's also unlikely that they will help you remember the successes of the session one month on. Tutors may find that they need to take responsibility for assisting the student with completing these records in the early stages. Later with increased confidence the student will take over this responsiblity. Good record keeping is embedded in the quality standards set out by the Basic Skills Agency's Quality Mark. Such records are also likely to be viewed by FEFC or OFSTED during an inspection. This underlines their importance for both the student and the tutor.

Lesson plans

For any learning session to be effective the tutor must plan in advance taking account of:

- available resources;
- the number of students;
- type of setting(1:1, group, open learning).

These factors will determine the type of lesson planning required.

Lesson plans should:

- give details of the activities and tasks the student/s are expected to cover;
- specify time allotted for each activity;
- describe methods and resources to be used;
- reflect the wider aims and specific goals of the student/s.

It is important to allow space to record items which need more practice and new areas of work which become apparent during the session.

Evaluating your teaching

New tutors often wonder, "How will I know if I'm getting it right?"

After a session a tutor may be surprised to find that things did not run according to plan. A piece of work may turn out to be harder and take a student longer than the time allotted on the session plan or a subject that the tutor thought would be relevant and interesting may evoke little response.

With increasing experience most tutors find ways of working flexibly to cope with the unexpected, but a good tutor will always ask, "Why did that happen?"

Whether new or established, all tutors should have a systematic way of examining their own performance. Five key questions can help you through this process.

1. Content – Am I focusing on the right things?

Remember, your teaching should link to the aims of the students' learning plans. When you make decisions on the learning outcomes for a particular session these plans should guide your choices.

2. Explanation – Do the students understand what to do and why they are doing it?

To get the most out of any activity the student needs to understand how it is going to help his learning. For instance, it may seem simple but pointless to underline all the words in a text that start with "ch" (chairman, character, charisma) unless the tutor explains that the ultimate purpose is to find words where the letters "c" "h" produce a different sound from "ch" as in "church".

3. Presentation – Were the methods and materials appropriate?

Was it at the right level of difficulty? Did the session go at a suitable pace? Was a variety of methods used? Were the materials interesting and relevant to the student?

4. Progress – How well did the session work?

What did people get out of it? What progress was made? Which of the learning outcomes were achieved?

How do you know this happened? How does the student know?

5. Future plans – Did you notice things that will need further work?

Did you make a note of these. As part of ongoing planning and review it is useful to record areas where more work is needed.

After looking at these five points the tutor should be in a good position to answer the question, 'How could I have improved that session: if I was running it again what changes would I make?' The organisation you are working for will probably have a checklist to help you assess how things are going. It may form part of the self-assessment model in preparation for inspection and could help you to identify any staff development or resource needs.

The tutor/student relationship

All tutors should periodically ask themselves the following questions.

- Have I made plans to defuse any anxieties that students might have?

- Do my teaching methods allow each student's previous experiences to be acknowledged and used?

- Is there a friendly working atmosphere?

- Do I make positive and constructive comments about each student's work/progress?

- Does the work allow students to see for themselves that they are making progress?

- Do I know what each student's long term goals are?

- Have I negotiated individual learning plans?

- Do I allow time for feedback and review within my sessions?

- Do I have a system for counselling/advising students whose individual goals or motivation are not being met or who are ready to move on?

4 | Practical Approaches

This section explores a wide range of learning methods and techniques. It describes the approaches used with each of the four students from *Part 2* – **Norma, Joe, Pat** and **Ansell**. It also suggests further activities which could be developed for individual or group work.

Case Study 1: **Norma**
Language experience (Matching and sequencing, Whole word recognition, Cloze procedure, Context cues, Language experience and EAL students) – The survival kit – A personal dictionary – Phonics – Key words – Alphabetical order – Social sight words – Handwriting – Beginning writing

---

Norma and her tutor began with the Language Experience Approach for teaching reading. This is the best method for beginners because it uses the student's own words and experiences. Texts are composed and then become a source for teaching reading, writing and spelling. The student feels more confident with such texts because the language and content is familiar.

Language experience

Norma is an excellent cook and makes wedding cakes for her friends and family. **Norma** and her tutor used this skill and experience as the basis for the Language Experience text. They talked about the cakes and the tutor wrote down some sentences. Once the sentences had been agreed upon, the tutor wrote a clear copy.

Some students may find it difficult to decide what to talk about but it's usually possible to write something even if it is just - "I don't know what to talk about." This will still give you some words to begin the method.

Don't change the language
It is important to keep to the student's own words and style. Don't insert, change or omit anything. If the student uses "was" instead of "were", or if singulars and plurals are mixed up, leave it as it is. That's not what you're dealing with at the moment and it would only cause a confusion to introduce these extra points.

31

Use short lines

Most sentences break naturally into phrases.

Norma's sentences were:

> I really like making wedding cakes
>
> I have an old recipe
>
> with butter, dried fruit
>
> and brandy.
>
> The best part
>
> is icing the layers
>
> and putting on the bride and groom.

Arranging the lines like this – called **'line-breaking'** – makes it easier for beginner readers because it gives them a chance to pause without losing the sense and allows them to tackle small bits at a time.

Norma's tutor read these sentences to her several times. Then she asked **Norma** to join in and read them together. This is sometimes referred to as **'shared reading'**. Gradually the tutor faded her voice out as **Norma** grew more confident. The words and content were familiar so if **Norma** had difficulty with a word, her tutor

32

encouraged reading on or recapping the sentence in order to foster prediction skills. If **Norma** was still unsure, her tutor gave the word immediately – support is very important at this stage. When **Norma** could read the piece confidently it was time to develop other activities from the text.

Language experience activities

A second copy of the reading text is needed for the further activities so that the student has a copy to refer to for help and checking.

1. Matching and sequencing

One text copy is cut into lines to match against the second copy. Then the student can practise putting the lines in the right sequence with and without the reference copy.

This is part of **Norma's** piece.

> The best part
>
> is icing the layers
>
> and putting on the bride and groom.

| is icing the layers | The best part | and putting on the bride and groom. |

2. Whole word recognition

Each sentence or line is taken separately and cut into individual words. The student matches the words to the reference copy, then sequences them in sentence order first with the copy, then without it.

One of **Norma's** sentences was:

| cakes. | I | really | like | wedding |

| making |

| I really like making wedding cakes. |

All the sentences/lines can be worked through in this way. The individual words become part of a "word bank" and can be used to make new sentences. The words should be kept in a useful way so that they can be added to and also used for revision. Plastic envelopes or box files can be used.

Whole word recognition is an important part of reading. A good sight vocabulary helps with the flow and meaning of a piece of reading.

There are several ways to practise whole word recognition.

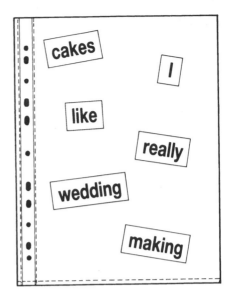

- Wordsearches

a	b	c	d	e	f	g
i	b	r	i	d	e	n
j	r	e	a	l	l	y
w	e	d	d	i	n	g
k	l	m	n	k	p	a
x	c	a	k	e	a	n
w	v	u	t	s	r	d

- Jigsaws

br	ide	mak	ing

- Bingo

like	part	I
best	cake	and

cake	the	is
I	and	part

- Pelmanism

Identical pairs of words turned face down and each player takes a turn trying to turn up a pair.

- Dominoes

I	cake

cake	like

like	and

- Labelling

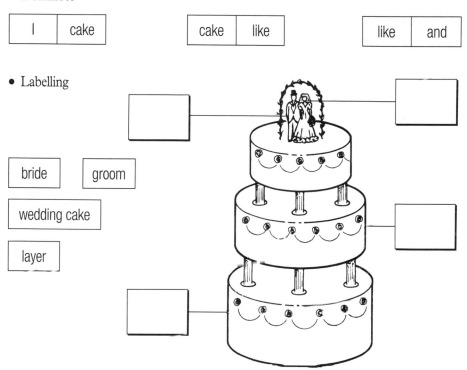

bride		groom

wedding cake

layer

3. Cloze procedure

Remove words from the text and ask the student to insert, predict or write in the missing words. This type of exercise is called a cloze exercise.

Norma's tutor made the following:

> I really like making..............................cakes.
>
> I have an .... recipe
>
> with butter, dried ....
>
> and brandy.
>
> The best ....
>
> is icing the layers
>
> .... putting on the bride and groom.

- Inserting words provides whole word practice too.

| old | fruit | part | wedding | and | groom |

- Writing the missing words in the cloze exercise introduces the student to spelling. Reading, writing and spelling should be taught together and should support each other. The beginner reader should be introduced to a spelling programme right from the start. Each week the student should work on 3 to 5 useful words following the **Look, Say, Cover, Write, Check** method which is discussed in detail on page 60.

When we read, we are getting the meaning from the words on the page. It doesn't matter if we can't read every word as we can omit the odd word and still get the gist of it. This is an activity that some people see as 'cheating' but, in fact, it is a strategy for coping with unknown words. The fluent reader probably uses this method more than any other.

You can take a passage and leave out some words and then work together to discuss the sort of words the writer might have used, bearing in mind that there are usually a number of possible answers.

Remember when preparing this activity do not delete too many words and leave the first sentence complete. The more words deleted, the more difficult it is to understand what's written.

Cloze is particularly useful for readers who are reluctant to read past an unknown word as it encourages them to read on and then guess the missing word.

You could also try the following with students.

- **Delete key words** – After he has identified the missing words, the student can practice writing and spelling them.

- **Omit words that contain the same sound** – You can set clues by discussing the writing and words first – or by providing certain letters in the word as well as the correct number of spaces. For example, using 'day' as the clue:

> We m _ _   have to   p _ _   to see the May D _ _   display.

4. Context cues – predicting

- In a group, students can write their own material, leaving out words for other students to guess. Predicting the missing words provides the student with practice in reading for meaning. It is a way to encourage the learner to guess unfamiliar or 'forgotten' words by using the context. The student should read forward or re-read part of the text to aid prediction. The student should also be encouraged to look for 'clues' from any pictures, headings and other features in the text layout. Predicting is a natural approach used by good readers.

Using the language experience approach with students whose first language is not English

When learning a language, listening and speaking come before reading and writing. Reading materials must therefore be within a student's own understanding of the language. This is particularly true in the early stages. Only when a student is a reasonably confident reader should new words be introduced through written text. It is important that reading is not an isolated activity but is closely related to and integrated with listening and speaking practice.

Language experience texts are particularly useful for this purpose. It ensures that the language is within a student's oral competence and that the subject matter is of relevance and interest. As described with the basic skills student, the tutor should agree the sentences to be written down, bearing in mind the level of competence in reading. It is also important with a second language student that any errors in the spoken language are discussed and corrected before the sentences are written down. There is no point in the second language learner reinforcing language errors by reading them.

Points to remember

1. You should explain to students what you are doing and why. Unless the students know the reason for doing a task, they are unlikely to be very interested in or to learn effectively from it. You will probably already know this from your own learning experiences.

2. From the beginning the student should be encouraged to use several techniques to work out unknown words:
   - leaving the word out and coming back to it;
   - guessing from the words around it and from his previous knowledge;
   - using the sounds as a clue.

Other practical approaches used with Norma

The survival kit

The tutor was very aware that **Norma** still had an extreme lack of confidence when it came to basic literacy skills. Whilst negotiating her learning plan, **Norma** and her tutor talked together about what would be a useful way to record what she was learning so that she could use new skills in practice outside the class. They came up with the idea of a 'survival kit'.

For this purpose, **Norma** would use an A5 size ring binder with subject dividers.

Different sections would allow her to look up:

- months of the year;
- days of the week;
- alphabet (upper and lower case);
- family names and addresses, telephone numbers and birthdays;
- social sight words;
- words needed for shopping/getting about;
- words for work;
- words for home.

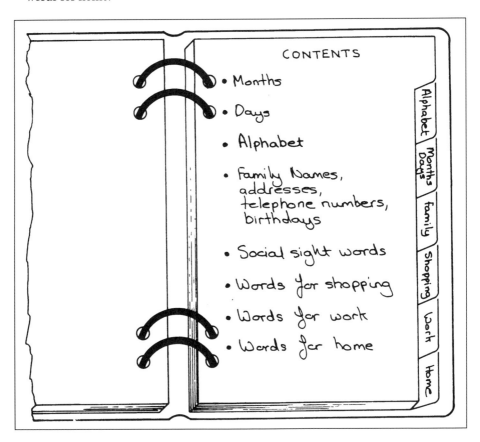

Planning out the survival kit and recording all the details provided a lot of work in itself and helped **Norma** to exercise her memory skills.

She needed a lot of help with organising and compiling the file initially, and found it was useful to use a highlighter pen to emphasise some words she found difficult. She also made use of pictures and colours to jog her memory. Looking things up in the survival kit proved to be an excellent form of revision.

There is a limit to what you can learn at once, especially when you lack confidence, so it is necessary to go over the same ground again and again with beginners. This type of file also helps the tutor – as it is a reminder of words and letter patterns the student is currently working on. It is essential when working with beginners, to be sensitive to what they are likely to know and what might cause difficulty.

After some time **Norma** and her tutor devised a follow-up to the survival kit. This dealt with **Norma's** immediate need to take over writing tasks which her husband had done previously.

This was organised into several sections.

Form filling
- Running a catalogue
- Post Office
- Coupons
- Paying and understanding bills

Grectings
- Birthdays
- Christmas
- Get well, etc.

Messages and Memos
- Milkman
- Work
- Friends/neighbours
- Abbreviations

Writing Cheques/Banking
- Current account
- Building Society account

Writing Letters
- Formal/informal

There were some things which she needed to tackle straight away, such as replying to formal letters from the Building Society and Bank. The tutor helped **Norma** to get together the information she needed and write out a formal reply for **Norma** to check through and sign. This meant the letter was dealt with, putting her mind at rest and giving her some sense of achievement which was very important at this stage.

Other tasks such as messages, memos and greetings, they could take more time over until **Norma** felt confident to use those sections of the survival kit on her own.

Suggestions on how to develop each of these areas of work can be found in other sections of the book.

Work which could be developed for an individual or a group

A personal dictionary

From the very beginning most tutors encourage students to keep a personal dictionary where new words they are learning can be added week by week. The personal dictionary may be simply a small note book with pages marked A-Z. Finding the appropriate pages gives practice in alphabetical order and also directs the student's attention to the word's initial sound.

Initial sounds

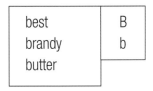

Students may think that recording the word in the book is the end of the process – you then have a growing body of words that you can refer to when needed. But it is important to realise that, at this stage, the word has not been *learned*. To be able to read or spell the new word confidently more work is required.

The personal dictionary notebook is meant to be used regularly in other ways. The student may use it for reading practice between sessions. The tutor may suggest particular spelling activities to be practised at home, with the dictionary as a reference list of words to work on. The student and tutor may decide on a particular page or pages as the focus work to be done, or the student may search the pages for words with identical letter patterns, e.g. mak<u>ing</u>, putt<u>ing</u>, wedd<u>ing</u>.

Word cards from earlier language experience work can be used along with the dictionary activities in matching and arranging words in alphabetical order. Some students get encouragement from a 'two envelopes system': the word cards are divided into 'words I am learning' and 'words I know', and with regular practice, the student sees cards move gradually from the first envelope to the second.

Phonics

It is useful for students to know initial sounds and common beginnings and endings of words. Sounds (phonics) help the student to guess some unknown words, and also help with some spellings. However, the relationship of sounds to letters is quite complicated, and not regular, so students should not be encouraged to concentrate on this method alone.

Reading should involve a combination of skills – whole word recognition, prediction and phonics.

Reading work involving sounds may be helped by matching and grouping activities. By concentrating on one sound, at the beginning, in the middle or at the end of words, a list of words can be produced. Make up some nonsense sentence with the student, for example:

> <u>N</u>ed is <u>n</u>ot my <u>n</u>ephew's name, my <u>n</u>ephew's <u>n</u>ame is <u>N</u>orman.
>
> The rai<u>n</u> i<u>n</u> Spai<u>n</u> falls mai<u>n</u>ly o<u>n</u> the plai<u>n</u>.

You can then cut up the sentences into individual words for various games – memory games, dominoes, bingo, snap – or simply sort them into groups and add more words. Try making up other nonsense sentences.

To be meaningful, the sounds need to be used as part of words and phrases.

Key words

These are small, common words that recur in all reading and writing. Although they are a relatively small group of words, they are particularly important and are difficult to learn by sounding out (try sounding out 'said' and 'they').

The following 32 words make up on average ⅓ of all the words we read or write.

a all and are as at be but for had have he him his I in is it not on of one said so that the they to was we with you

Along with these additional words, the total 100 words make up on average ½ of all the words we read or write.

about an back been before big by call came can come could did do down first from get go has her here if into just like little look made make me more much must my new no now off old only or other our out over right see she some their them then there this two up want well went were what when where which who will you

---

from J. McNally & W. Murray, *Key Words and Literacy and the Teaching of Reading*, Schoolmaster Publishing

41

Alphabetical order

The ability to recite the alphabet from A-Z is only of limited value when trying to use a telephone directory or a dictionary. However in order to locate information which is stored alphabetically, it is essential to know where letters stand in relation to one another.

As soon as a working knowledge of order has been established, use it in realistic situations. Work with telephone directories, street guides, indices and dictionaries, after all, they are the reason for learning alphabetical order in the first place.

Some useful activities for teaching alphabetical order are:

- give a few letter cards to be sorted into order, for example, d c e b a, and random letters, not in immediate sequence, for example, v, r, p, n (do not use the whole alphabet to begin with);

- give a word in code, where the student has to find the word by using the next letter of the alphabet, for example, sghr (= this);

- practise finding a particular letter in a dictionary, using the top corner as a guide. If you open the dictionary at m and you are looking for s, do you move forward or back, and how far;

- play 'sevens' with letter cards. One set of alphabet playing cards are all dealt out. The person with m starts, and each player in turn can lay one card down if they have the next one in sequence either forwards or backwards;

- use filing cards, as in a filing system, to reinforce and extend early work. It is a simple matter to build up a filing system which can be extended as confidence grows, to include words filed by 2nd and 3rd letters, etc.

All these activities should be made self checking by providing a copy of the alphabet.

Social sight words

REMEMBER - beginning readers are not beginning thinkers.

Adults who say they can't read, can often recognise many of the words they see everyday in shops, on the street, on television and in the papers. Each person has a

slightly different group of words, though some are common to us all – EXIT, ENTRANCE, NO SMOKING, etc. They are words which are more often read than written. Tutors can write the sight words the student wants to remember onto flash cards.

Recognising many sight words depends on the style they are written in.

Some signs are written in capital letters or use a particular typographical style. However it is interesting to note that signs and notices are increasingly being written in lower case rather than block capitals.

It is often helpful if students can see signs in their appropriate context, e.g.

Dairy Products	⬆
Confectionery	⬆
Biscuits	➡
Frozen Foods	⬊

Handwriting

The amount of work that needs to be done on handwriting will depend on the writer's ability. Some students' writing is fine and they are quite happy with the presentation. Others worry that their handwriting shows their lack of ability in reading and writing. To cope with each situation, you need to know the student's feelings about his own writing in order to offer the most appropriate support. You also need to ensure the students can read what you write.

Some habits will be hard to break and you need to consider whether it is necessary to do so. Will forming a certain letter the "wrong" way make it more tiring for the student, if he is writing for any length of time? Might his way make the learning of joined writing more complicated?

As much as possible, work from the students' knowledge and build on it. Encourage proof reading in order to pick out features which need to be improved.

Only in circumstances where the formation of the letters is getting in the way of the real reasons for writing, i.e. to communicate, should you consider altering radically the way the student writes.

For a student who writes well but is not happy with the style, it might be useful to collect together a wide variety of examples of handwriting from tutors. The student may then begin to see that his own style is no less legible than most people's.

By not starting to alter someone's handwriting immediately, you may find that he alters it himself just by doing more writing.

A student who is a beginning reader and writer may use large and small letters indiscriminately. Is this due to nerves? Is the student unaware of the use of capital (upper case) and small (lower case) letters? Does the student have difficulty in discriminating between the lower case **b** and **d** or **p** and **q** so uses the upper case equivalents? What about the spacing between words? Having sorted out the answers to these questions and others that you have in mind, a few activities need to be planned. They might include some of the following:

- write out a reference alphabet in large (upper case) and small (lower case) letters, for example,

$$Aa, \quad Bb$$

- work on one group of letters that derive from one basic shape, for example,

$$c \quad c \quad a \quad d \quad e \quad g \quad o \quad q$$

These letters can then be used to form words that the student can trace and write below. Make sure the writing lines are not too close together. Encourage the students to over emphasise the size of the letters to begin with in order to feel the shape of the letter.

- Do matching activities for upper and lower case letters – individual letters on cards, handwritten, typed, Letraset, etc. Ask the student to write down letters in small or capital letters which can then be checked from cards.

It is important to encourage joined writing from the early stages because it helps the student to remember the flow of letters and the pattern of the word, and so is a useful skill for learning spellings.

- For joined writing, some basic patterns could be introduced to help the student feel the flow of the shapes. Use a variety of writing materials – pencils, felt-tip, plain paper, wide lined paper, etc.

Beginning writing

First thing for beginner writers

Start with the thing which is most important for the student. If there is something you have an urgent reason to write you are more likely to practise to get it right.

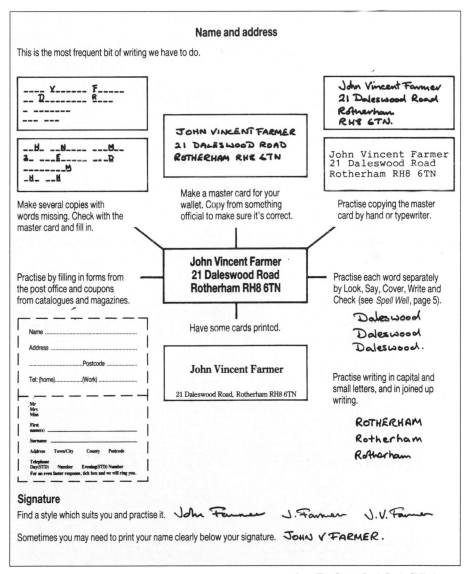

Name and address

This is the most frequent bit of writing we have to do.

Make several copies with words missing. Check with the master card and fill in.

Make a master card for your wallet. Copy from something official to make sure it's correct.

Practise copying the master card by hand or typewriter.

Practise by filling in forms from the post office and coupons from catalogues and magazines.

**John Vincent Farmer
21 Daleswood Road
Rotherham RH8 6TN**

Practise each word separately by Look, Say, Cover, Write and Check (see *Spell Well*, page 5).

Have some cards printed.

John Vincent Farmer

21 Daleswood Road, Rotherham RH8 6TN

Practise writing in capital and small letters, and in joined up writing.

Signature

Find a style which suits you and practise it.

Sometimes you may need to print your name clearly below your signature.

from *The Starter Pack*, Basic Skills Agency

Writing cheques

Nowadays wages are often paid by cheque or straight into a bank account. Therefore it is important to feel confident about using a cheque book to pay for things.

A cheque is just a signed instruction from you to the bank. But the layout of a cheque can be confusing.

The things you need to write correctly are:

- the date – in figures or words
- the name of the person you want to pay – the payee
- the amount you want to pay – in words and figures
- the word 'only' after the pounds if no pence are added
- your signature – which may be matched with your cheque card.

| Counterfoil cheque stub to keep for your records | Payee – name of person you want to pay | Amount in words | Amount in numbers | Date | Bank sort code |

| cheque numbers | Bank and branch number (sort code) | Lines showing a crossed cheque | Your account number | Your name and signature |

To make sure that your cheque is accepted you will need to sign it. In a shop you will usually be asked to show a cheque card, or banker's card. Your signature will be matched against this card. You can apply for a cheque card if you have a bank account – cards are issued to 'reliable' customers!

Does your signature look the same every time?

Other things you will need to learn are the various ways in which dates can be written, e.g. 24th April 1991; 24/4/91; April 24. '91
Try writing these dates various ways.

24th December 1998 ....

1st April 1987 ....

1st January 1999 ....

8/6/99 ....

20/11/98 ....

15/8/99 ....

from *The Starter Pack*, Basic Skills Agency

Messages and memos

When writing notes we are concerned to communicate main ideas and to record the maximum amount of information in the minimum number of words.

- Frequently notes are to members of our family, the milkman, or for ourselves. These can be very cryptic – 'Back at 6' – '2 pints please' – and tend to pose few problems with practice.

- Other more formal notes are simply brief letters and can be usefully introduced as passages to be completed, for example, a letter of absence from school.

Dear..

....will not be at school

as she..

Yours sincerely,

....

- Taking telephone messages is frequently unnerving for many people. This may not simply be a matter of jotting down the main points but can involve difficulty with spelling names, addresses, etc. Students may need to be reassured that it is perfectly alright to ask spellings - 'Sorry, I didn't catch that name. Could you spell it please?'

- Making notes at meetings is a more complex activity. However, practice can be gained by starting with simple exercises and gradually increasing the difficulty. It may be helpful to tape record role-play sessions of meetings because in this way the main points contained in the notes can be checked with the original discussions. Students should be encouraged to omit inessential words as well as points which are peripheral to the main argument. As soon as possible the notes should be written up in order that the gist of what has been said is still fresh in the mind. Reporting back from notes gives an idea of whether they are full enough or not.

Messages and memos

A message or a memo can be short and sharp as long as it includes the essential information. Someone else will read it so it must be clear.

If you are taking a telephone message:

- don't write everything the caller says
- pick out the important points
- remember to make a note of names, dates and times.

To _Lena_
11.15 am Mon.
Jeff (from Personnel) rang.
Manager bringing visitors
to see production line.
4.30 today.
_V._ Important   Be prepared!
                              Sue.

Some offices have their own special memo pads which you should learn to use.

MESSAGES	THINGS TO DO TODAY
To	
Date .... Time	
Signed	
A&B BUILDERS LIMITED 4 Roach Road, Rotherham, Yorkshire	**ANCHOR OIL COMPANY** Oil Rig House, Sloane Road, Reading, Berks.

Post-it - Telephone Message Pad 7660

To _____
Date _____
Time _____
WHILE YOU WERE OUT
M _____
of _____
Phone No. _____
TELEPHONED
WAS IN TO SEE YOU
WANTS TO SEE YOU   PLEASE CALL
RETURNED YOUR CALL   WILL CALL BACK
Message _____   **URGENT**
_____
_____
FT 5001-6785-1
Operator _____

Learn some useful abbreviations.

Mon	Aug	am	eg
Tues	Sep	pm	etc
Wed	Oct	N.B.	p.s.

Make a Select-a-Message and practise writing the various combinations.

To the ....

Milkman, Paperboy, baker, etc.

Please leave ....

3 pints, The Times, ½ doz eggs, 2 large brown

On ....

Monday afternoon, the back doorstep Tuesday evening the kitchen window sill

Thank you.

For further practice, tape record a variety of personal and business messages which the student can listen to and write.

from *The Starter Pack*, Basic Skills Agency

Joe was able to identify several areas of reading which he wanted to concentrate on. He urgently needed some help with the union correspondence. At the same time he wanted to review his personal financial position in case he lost his job. With a mortgage, personal pension and various insurance policies he received frequent statements and mailings about 'special' or 'free' offers. Many of these were written in language which seemed designed to confuse and this had led in the past to him unwittingly signing agreements for unwanted items or increased contributions. He needed to learn some ways to identify the main points in these types of letters and how to summarize their contents.

Extending reading techniques

Joe is not a bad reader. He can de-code words but doesn't feel he gets much out of his reading. He needs to move from being a mechanical reader to being an effective reader where he is constantly reading for meaning.

In his new role of shop steward he constantly receives minutes of union meetings which he needs to read accurately so that he can report back to his work mates. Although he has usually been in attendance at these meetings and is therefore aware of what has happened, he is not using this prior knowledge to help him understand the minutes to be read. **Joe** and his tutor talked about his particular reading difficulties and decided that reading these minutes would be a good way to improve his comprehension skills.

1. It was agreed that before reading the minutes with his tutor, **Joe** would relate what he already knew about the meeting – topics discussed, people present, decisions taken, and list these.

2. The tutor then divided the minutes into more manageable chunks so that it didn't look like a solid block of text (see example overleaf).

3. **Joe** would then:

   a. start reading a sentence at a time;

   b. try to guess unknown words using his prior knowledge and context clues. If needed, look at the initial letter for additional help;

   c. try to spot inconsistencies in meaning if he gives a nonsense substitution;

   d. be given the correct word if still struggling;

	MAIN POINTS
J.V. who led the union delegation reported on the latest talks with management held last week. This had proved to be a lengthy and at times acrimonious meeting with little consensus emerging.	Long meeting No agreement
J.V. had yet again presented our case for an across the board 12% increase, back dated to April, based on cost of living increases and rises in productivity by our members already conceded by management.	Our Claim 12% from April
They as usual repeated their last offer of 6% for the lowest paid only and 5.3% for supervisory grades. Even this was made conditional on a review of staffing levels throughout the factory.	Their offer 6% low paid 5.3% supervisors with strings
After several hours of talks during which we continued to present our case forcibly there was some movement on their side with an increase in their offer of 1% for the low paid subject to a reduction in holiday entitlement.	Upped to 7% for low paid
This was clearly unacceptable and the meeting broke up with no agreement in sight.	Not acceptable

e. repeat phrases where he has had problems to help him extract meaning from the text;

f. recap at the end of the sentence - ask himself what it was about and check that it agrees with what he already knows about the meeting;

g. at the end of each chunk of text, list the main points.

4. When he has finished, comparison of the two lists (before and after) should show him how successfully he has been able to apply his existing knowledge to making sense of the reading.

To enable **Joe** to handle his personal correspondence, a monthly diary was created. Bills, pension, insurance and mortgage statements could be entered. When each was received, significant words and phrases were highlighted using coloured pens and **Joe** was encouraged to try and draw out the main points in each letter as he did with the union minutes. His tutor used some of these letters to show **Joe** how important it was to 'read between the lines' to try and discover why a letter had been sent.

Opposite is part of a letter received from an insurance company. Together **Joe** and the tutor looked at the purpose of this letter. Had it been sent merely to enclose a statement or did the writer have another purpose in mind? What effect does the letter have on the reader? Are particular words and phrases used deliberately to achieve this effect? Is it typical of other letters he has received from insurance companies?

Dear Mr

YOU COULD BE MAKING MORE OF YOUR <u>NEW</u> TAX-FREE ALLOWANCE

I have great pleasure in enclosing your annual statement with details of your investment.

You already appreciate the importance of saving for the future and know that the tax-free savings in a Friendly Society have greater growth potential than savings in a comparable plan which is subject to tax.

Good news is that <u>you can now benefit from even higher tax free savings than those you currently enjoy.</u>

In the last budget, the chancellor increased your tax-free savings limits to £18 a month, £200 a year or £1,600 for lump sum investors. It makes sound financial sense to take advantage of this new......

Points to notice

1. The tutor and **Joe** talked a lot about his particular reading difficulties. They had discussed his reading style and analysed the strategies he used when reading. It was as a result of this discussion that they agreed to look at 'reading for meaning'.

2. Everything was based on what the student wanted to read. To develop reading with understanding **Joe** needed to be using texts which were of some purpose to him and took into account his interests and the knowledge he already possessed.

3. Pre-reading activities such as talking about the meeting before reading the minutes can be as important as the actual reading of the text and encourage the reader to question what he is reading.

4. All of the techniques used aim to create an active involvement in the reading process so that **Joe** can make reading meaningful for himself and develop his reading strategies independently of his tutor.

Work which could be developed for an individual or a group

Hearing reading

If you are to discover the reading style of your student you need to listen to the student reading aloud. This may be an awkward experience for your student and you need to discuss together the purpose of this activity – to provide information about the strategies used when reading and so enable tutor and student to plan useful reading activities.

To make the situation less stressful the student could, in private, read a text on to tape and then with the tutor play the tape back and discuss the strategies used. This enables the student to gain insight into the techniques he uses in de-coding text.

After you have analysed a student's reading style it is not necessary to always hear them reading. The tutor can check if they've understood a passage through asking questions, discussion or written tasks. However, many students feel they need the tutor to listen to them reading to check that they are getting it right. This need should not be ignored. It can also be useful for the tutor to read to the student, although this is more common at Entry Level. This can help the student to follow and enjoy a story.

Skimming

A lot of adult reading is done in this way. It consists of glancing through a piece of text to get a general idea of what it is about. You could practice this with the student by using some of the following:

- read a short paragraph and suggest a title;

- read a newspaper article and note down the main points;

- discuss features in the text which help you to skim – e.g. headings, paragraphs, words in bold type or italics.

Scanning

Here the reader is looking for specific information in the text. Irrelevant details are disregarded and attention is focused on particular key words. This is a very important skill to acquire since it is related to a lot of adult reading tasks. You can often practise it by:

- asking students to find particular entries in a telephone directory or timetable;

- posing questions asking for particular detail from a short text.

Using a dictionary

Students are often wary of using a dictionary, being unsure of how to find their way round or of becoming confused with phonetic spellings, notes about derivation and small print. You could try some of the following with students.

- Look at a number of different dictionaries to compare size of print, layout, etc. People tend to have their personal preferences, so let the students select the one they find easier to use.

- Spend time getting to know a particular dictionary. Find the page which explains the meaning of any abbreviations used. Look up some words that the students already know to make sure they understand the system.

- Practise alphabetical order by finding a particular letter in the dictionary, using the top corner as a guide. If you open the dictionary at **p** and you are looking for **w** do you move forward or back, and how far?

- Produce word cards to be put in alphabetical order:

– with different 1st letters;

tin

book		nation

group

– with the same first letter;

book

big		bell

band

– with the same first two letters;

brown

bread		brand

brick

– with the same first three letters.

brown

brother		broad

broken

Letter writing

A letter always has a purpose, which is closely reflected in the style. These two aspects, purpose and style, should be considered together. It is usually helpful to discuss these aspects and perhaps to work out and compose a letter orally before writing it. This can also form a useful group activity, a student or tutor acting as note-taker for the group's ideas.

Correspondence to friends or relatives, postcards, greetings on special occasions, many invitations, etc. are expressions of personal messages and are therefore written in a spontaneous informal style. The message itself is more important than the way in which it is conveyed. This kind of letter writing is an ideal way of encouraging students to record events of individual significance, convey feelings or state opinions. Development of technical skills like spelling can then be based on this writing.

Letters ordering goods, asking for or giving information, querying or complaining, are in most cases written to people we only know in an official or professional capacity, if at all. It may be important to make a good impression both by what we say and the way we present ourselves. One of the ways of doing this is to observe the set conventions of formal letter writing:

- lay-out;

address of sender
date
address of person sent to
beginning
ending

correctly placed on the page

- correct spelling and punctuation;

- conventions of expression which include:

Beginnings – *Dear Sir,* (to a company or organisation),
Dear Mr./Mrs./Ms. (to someone we do not know well but whose name we know);

Endings – *Dear Sir,* ends *Yours faithfully,*
Dear Mr./Mrs./Ms. ends *Yours sincerely.*

The content of a formal letter should be stated clearly, simply and concisely, in language as natural as possible. To do this, the writer needs to be quite clear about what he wishes to say. This may involve quite a lot of discussion beforehand and is likely to involve drafting, redrafting and making a fair copy. You may like to try some of the following activities with students:

- practise different ways of writing the date;

- practise writing out addresses, paying particular attention to punctuation and the way it is set out;

- practise laying out a letter on letter blanks (with layout lines already ruled in to create a strong visual impression of the shape of a letter);

- re-order jumbled paragraphs into a logical sequence;

- fill in 'guided' letters in which certain parts have been omitted for the student to fill in. (This is a useful exercise in a mixed level group, as more or less may be omitted from individual letters);

- group a jumbled list of sentences from two different letters (possibly in two different styles) into sentences appropriate to individual letters;

- match letters with their answers;

- practise writing birthday cards and postcards;

- keep an individual file of 'model letters' which may come in useful;

- compose a letter together, tutor and student, or the whole group.

Case Study 3 – **Patricia**
Extending writing (drafting and editing) – Improving spelling – Punctuation

---

Patricia was keen to gain qualifications and her long term goal was to take a GCSE English course aiming for a C grade or above. Whilst her work in classes had enabled her to gain the confidence needed to deal effectively with everyday writing tasks, for example letter writing, she struggled with longer writing assignments of the type required for GCSE work.

An extract from **Patricia's** new learning plan

LEARNING PLAN CAMBRIAN ADULT EDUCATION CENTRE		Student Copy
PATRICIA		
Your plan for the next 6 weeks **SUMMER TERM – 2nd half**	Half-time review ✔ ⟶ ✗	Further plan **SUMMER TERM – 2nd half**
Topics to be covered **Letter – writing** **1) recap on layout of formal letter** **2) shorter letters – to nursery – buying by post** **3) longer letters – complaining job applications** **4) Spelling strategies**	 ✔ ✔ ✔ ⟶ ⟶	**Look at longer pieces of writing where ideas need to be developed** **Develop editing and drafting skills** **extended letter – writing skills** **keep up regular practice**
Anything else? Individual needs **Qualifications important. Aim for GMOCF Level 2**		**Move into sort of writing tasks needed for course work GCSE**
How's it going? **More confident about my spelling though not perfect. Punctuation a problem. Writing a long piece is still hard.**		

56

In her new learning plan it was decided that **Patricia** needed to develop her confidence with these longer pieces and that work on drafting and editing skills could assist her in this. Whilst she was more confident about her spelling, it was by no means perfect and still caused her some anxiety. She had also become aware that her punctuation could be improved.

The primary goal of this work was to enable **Patricia** to get her ideas down on paper with confidence, rather than aiming at perfection in spelling and punctuation before attempting to tackle this form of writing. These aspects could be dealt with separately.

Extending writing

The approach used was to encourage her to express herself in writing using drafting and editing techniques as the tool.

Choosing a subject to write about like 'childhood memories', meant that **Patricia** could concentrate on expressing herself effectively in writing and in beginning to develop her own writing style. The actual content, ie. her memory, was familiar and therefore had only to be 'recalled' rather than 'invented' as would be the case with other assignments.

The following are the stages **Patricia** used in the production of this writing:

1. discussion within her group;

2. getting her ideas down on paper, not worrying about spelling or punctuation;

Extract A

During the summer months we would make are own girders as we used to call them they were made out of old prams that people had thrown away we did not use all the pram just the weals then we attached a plank of wood and a piece of string to the front of it this was so we cloudster it then we would take them and have race down the brow this was steep and the only way to stop was to put your feet on the ground but if you were going to fast this meant you went over the top and landed in a pile of bricks and bracken glass they were because of the demalistion.

Extract B

In thoughs days you had to go round in a gang as this was saver than being on you own the gang consisted of brothers and sisters except one this was Pip his sister was to young to come with us. The others in the gang were Jacky and Steven they lived on the same side as Pip were as Malcom and Debby and Noel and I lived on the opposite side to them. Jacky had long blond hear and ware it in a pony tale her brother Steven had short trousers. Malcom had red hear and freckles and so did his sister Debby Noel had short brown hear and I had shoulder length hear.

---

3. reading back what she had written, checking to see if she had missed anything out, checking if it made sense;

4. reading together with tutor or to group members. Punctuation errors may well be corrected at this point as reading aloud often highlights where such errors interfere with the sense of the passage. Correct spellings can be given as necessary;

5. getting suggestions for working on any problem areas e.g. clarification of confusing bits, deletion of repetitions;

Re-drafted Extract B

In those days you had to go round in a gang as this was safer than being on your own. The members of our gang were myself, my younger brother Noel, Malcolm and his sister Debby, Jacky and her elder brother Steven and Pip who was the odd one out because his sister was too young to join the gang. We lived on either side of the street. I was the quiet one, my brother Noel was mischievous and played tricks on us all. Malcolm and his sister Debby had red hair and freckles we some times could not tell them apart. Jacky had long blond hair and wore it in a pony tale. Steven had short hair. Pip had dirty blond hair and always wore short trousers being the youngest of all could get away with doing something wrong whereas we could not.

---

6. redrafting;

7. re-reading and if happy with the sense and the content then look in more detail at punctuation and spelling.

Final Extract B

In those days you had to go round in a gang as this was safer than being on your own. The members of our gang were myself, my younger brother Noel, Malcolm and his sister Debby, Jacky and her elder brother Steven and Pip who was the odd one out because his sister was too young to join the gang. We lived on either side of the street. I was the quiet one, my brother Noel was mischievous and played tricks on us all. Malcolm and his sister Debby had red hair and freckles: we sometimes could not tell them apart. Jacky had long blond hair and wore it in a pony tail. Her brother Steven had short blond hair. Pip had dirty blond hair and always wore short trousers. Being the youngest of the gang he could get away with doing something wrong, whereas we could not.

Points to notice

Discussion can be an important part of the writing process. Listening to and sharing memories with one other person, say the tutor, or the group serves not only to aid recall but allows the subject matter to be tried before an audience prior to committing anything to paper. Positive responses from group members are of immeasurable value in boosting confidence and in helping students to move from having the ideas in their head to actual writing. Never underestimate how difficult and frightening a task this is for the new writer.

Spelling work is best dealt with after the final draft stage. For an example of such work see below in the spelling section.

Punctuation is often viewed as a goal in itself. Reading aloud is a good way of helping the student to realise that punctuation is a mechanism to make sense of the passage and is used and controlled by the writer. It is not a set of rules to be learnt and rigidly applied. It is possible to complete punctuation exercises correctly and still not be able to transfer this skill to your own writing.

The importance of, and necessity to make drafts cannot be stressed enough. Students often assume that good writers get it right first time, that they produce pieces of writing without error automatically.

Students view drafting and crossing out as evidence of failure rather than as an accepted part of the writing process which good writers utilise. For this reason many students use the computer or word processor to help them draft and proof read. This allows them to make corrections before the final paper copy emerges.

It is sometimes better to read the material with the student to discuss together problem areas rather than taking away material and returning it marked and altered for the student. Often students will know that something is not quite right with the writing, but will find it difficult to identify exactly what is wrong and how to remedy it themselves. Suggestions from the tutor are therefore very useful at this stage.

Work which could be developed for an individual or a group

Improving spelling

Before working on spelling students need to understand:

- that reading and spelling are different skills. Doing more reading will not necessarily improve your ability to remember spellings;
- that spelling is a skill you learn by writing – if you don't write regularly your spelling won't improve;
- that good spellers use a variety of strategies to learn words – any strategy that works is acceptable;
- that spelling is largely a visual skill. This means that students need to know when a word looks right.

As with reading, tutors need to start by talking with their students about the words they want to use and the type of mistakes they make. Only after such discussion can you identify suitable strategies to fit the learning style of the student.

Spellings to be learnt need to be taken from a student's writing, or from words identified as important by a student (e.g. words to do with a car from a student's motor vehicle course). You also need to be realistic about how many words can be learnt at any one time. After this you need to choose a suitable method.

1. For remembering whole words, you should use the **Look/Say/Cover/Write/Check** method. Write the word down, then:
   - **look** at the word try and picture it in your mind;
   - **say** the word out loud;
   - **cover** the word up;
   - **write** the word;
   - **check** that the word is correct.

Repeat the process 24 hours and 2 or 3 days after that.

2. Build up your knowledge of prefixes and suffixes.

   appear   **dis**appear   **dis**appear**ance**

3. Look at letter patterns – present the words in groups containing the same pattern.

   s**ight**   e**ight**   he**ight**

Sometimes groups of words can be presented that have spellings that reflect their meaning.

   opti**cian**   musi**cian**   techni**cian**.

Here identical visual patterns, are the important feature – not similar sound patterns.

4. Develop and use memory techniques to fix difficult spellings.

   I.C.I. make med**ici**ne.   Ne**cess**ary has one **c**ollar and two **s**leeves.

For this to be successful the student has to understand the technique used or develop their own.

5. Break words into syllables. This enables you to break long words up and concentrate on one bit at a time.

   in / de / pend / ence

Words that are being learnt can be recorded in a personal dictionary for reference and revision.

Word	1st try	24 hours later	3 days later
point	point	pont point	point
ap|point	appoint	appoint	appoint
here t|here	her here there	here there	here there

Spelling rules

Most students will want to learn rules that they believe will help them with their spelling. There are a number of rules: not all of them are useful. For example, the rule **'when two vowels walk together, the first one does the talking'** is designed to help with words like *goat, beam, rain*, etc. However, some of the most common words flout this rule, e.g. *said, could* and in the rule itself, *does*. Even so, some rules can help a lot, for example, on doubling letters, or changing the **y** at the end of a word to **–ies** in the plural. Students need to try them out to see if they make sense to them. Remember when teaching students spelling rules e.g. **'I before E except after C'**, that it is important to point out that all rules have exceptions – s**ei**ze, prot**ei**n, etc.!

Punctuation

As with other stages in the writing process the tutor needs to talk with the student and use their writing to discover what problems they might be having with punctuation. Make sure you discuss the purpose of punctuation, which is to help the writer to get their message across.

For the Entry Level student the use of full stops and capital letters can be introduced straight away. These simply set markers for the start and end of statements. You can move on to look at sentences which are questions and show the mark used at the end of these sentences.

Later commas and quotation marks can he taught followed by other forms of punctuation such as colons and semi colons.

Try some of the following with the students.

- Passages can be read for meaning and then afterwards be read looking at the punctuation used. You can discuss the effect particular marks have on the meaning of the passage.

- Sentences can be read out loud to illustrate the effect of punctuation on the intonation as well as the meaning, for example:

  - Go home (by taxi)   • Go home!   • Go home?

For further practice, sample passages can be re-written leaving out most of the punctuation. The student can then add the punctuation he thinks appropriate and check his version with the original. The differences – not always errors – can form the basis for discussion.

> *Case Study 4:* **Ansell**
> **Learning support – Vocationally based work – Forms**

Learning support

Ansell's tutor said:

'**Ansell** was very nervous about coming for learning support. He didn't want the other catering students to find out that he was having extra help and he was quite defensive.
   We talked through the things that were causing him difficulties and made a list:

- note taking in class;
- new, unfamiliar words;
- a bit slow at copying;   } now
- organising his studying;
- spelling;

- taking down phone messages;   } future
- filling in order forms.

Ansell thought his reading was all right as long as he wasn't rushed. To get a more objective view I asked him to try two cloze exercises from Judy Vaughan's pack, *Assessing Reading.*'

62

As **Ansell** says:

'I had to look through two pages on catering and fill in some of the blank spaces. It wasn't really a test, more like a puzzle to guess the missing words.'

From the answers he gave the tutor showed **Ansell** how they could work out his present reading level so they would know where to start.

Vocationally based

They decided to concentrate first on the catering vocabulary that **Ansell** found unfamiliar.

Glossary of terms

With the help of the catering tutor, we compiled a list of words and meanings which **Ansell** kept handy for quick reference in his catering course folder. He could use this to speed up his note taking in class as the list provided a reminder of the words and how to spell them.

Abbreviations

Ansell knew that there were short ways of writing some words (like 'bec.' for 'because') and had tried to use this for himself but could not always read back his notes as his system was haphazard. We started by learning a few common abbreviations and Ansell agreed to stick to these until others were gradually introduced.

Study skills

Once **Ansell's** course notes went into his catering folder he seemed to think the work was done. I explained a bit about how memory works and we talked about ways of organising and revising his notes. Through re-reading and discussion he began to see how to pick out the main points and we then marked those in some way.

Highlighting

'Sometimes I use a highlighter pen on important words or I underline the main headings. Sometimes I draw a circle or a square around a particular section or I number the different parts like a list. Then when I look back at my notes I can see which bits to go over.'

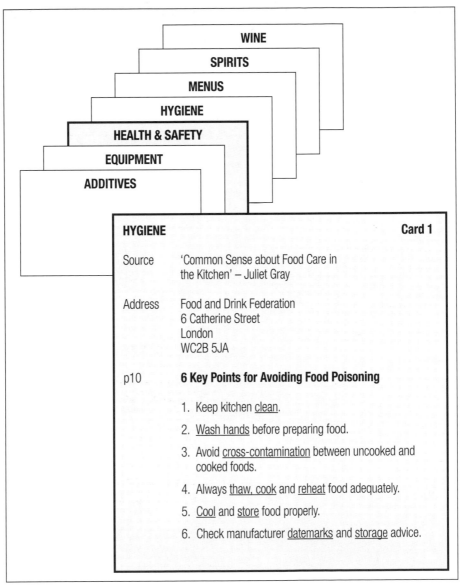

WINE

SPIRITS

MENUS

HYGIENE

HEALTH & SAFETY

EQUIPMENT

ADDITIVES

| HYGIENE | Card 1 |

Source — 'Common Sense about Food Care in the Kitchen' – Juliet Gray

Address — Food and Drink Federation
6 Catherine Street
London
WC2B 5JA

p10 — **6 Key Points for Avoiding Food Poisoning**

1. Keep kitchen <u>clean</u>.

2. <u>Wash hands</u> before preparing food.

3. Avoid <u>cross-contamination</u> between uncooked and cooked foods.

4. Always <u>thaw, cook</u> and <u>reheat</u> food adequately.

5. <u>Cool</u> and <u>store</u> food properly.

6. Check manufacturer <u>datemarks</u> and <u>storage</u> advice.

An example from Ansell's card index

Card index

Building up a card index is a useful way of sorting and storing information. **Ansell's** learning support tutor suggested he kept a card index to help him with future assignments and revision. Together they went through his catering course notes and decided on topic headings. These were written on the top line of each card and arranged alphabetically in an index card box. So that **Ansell** could easily refer back to his course notes or the material he had read, they decided to carefully note the source and page number of the information he summarised on the cards. Useful addresses were also noted. In order to help him remember the different points, key words were underlined. They also discussed using colour.

Ansell developed his card index system and eventually used it to help him gain Wordpower Stage 2 Unit 014 Element 2 'Create a reference system for a particular purpose'.

Assignments – reading textual and graphical material

On many courses students have to cope with tables and diagrams as well as text. When **Ansell** was asked to do an assignment on 'Christmas Catering: the dangers' he came to his basic skills support tutor for help. He had been able to collect a lot of useful information. This included pamphlets and graphs but he did not know how to relate one to the other, or how to divide his assignment into different sections. First they decided to mark all the possible useful information with a star ★, then they decided to divide it into one of three categories: The Facts 'F', The Dangers 'D', and The Signs 'S'.

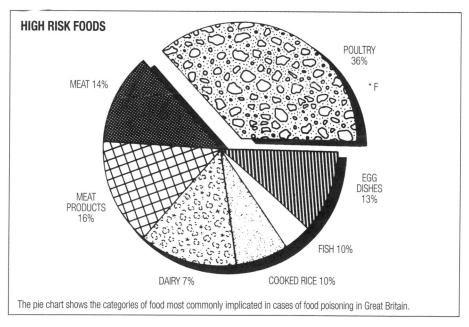

HIGH RISK FOODS

POULTRY 36%
* F
MEAT 14%
MEAT PRODUCTS 16%
EGG DISHES 13%
FISH 10%
DAIRY 7%
COOKED RICE 10%

The pie chart shows the categories of food most commonly implicated in cases of food poisoning in Great Britain.

from *Materials Pack & User Guide for Modular Delivery of Wordpower/Numberpower*, Alpha Flexible Learning

What causes food poisoning?

Food poisoning usually results from eating food contaminated with large numbers of micro-organisms or 'germs' as they may be known or the toxins (poisons) produced by them.

Some foods may be contaminated with germs when they enter the home; others may become contaminated in the home. So how does contamination and/or the undesirable growth of 'germs' occur in the home.

There are few people who wouldn't raise their hands in horror at the thought of their kitchens being a breeding ground for 'germs' - but the simple fact is that the world around us is full of 'germs' of one set or another (with some we live in harmony, others can be harmful).

As far as food poisoning 'germs' are concerned the main culprits are bacteria and/or the toxins they produce with salmonella bacteria being one of the most common.

SOURCES OF SALMONELLA

Meat, mainly poultry, is the most common source of salmonella. Many a Christmas has been ruined because the turkey has not been properly thawed and cooked or not properly stored after cooking.

Other sources are the faeces of an infected human or animal, unwashed hands, flies, mice and even household pets. All can transfer bacteria to the food we eat.

SOURCES OF OTHER BACTERIA

Other food poisoning bacteria e.g. staphylococci can be found on the skin especially in cuts and boils or in the nose. It is an easy matter for food to become contaminated when it is touched by dirty hands or when sneezed or coughed upon.

MOULDS

Visible mould growth on food is a sign that the food has been badly stored and that food poisoning bacteria might have had a chance to grow. Therefore foods should always be stored under the right conditions to prevent them going mouldy (check the label for storage instructions). Food which has gone mouldy should be thrown away

MOULDS LOVE . . .
● **Bread and Cakes**
● **Cheese**
● **Jams and Marmalades**

THE GOOD NEWS . . .

IN ORDER TO GROW, ALL BACTERIA AND MOULDS NEED THE RIGHT DEGREE OF TEMPERATURE AND TIME AND MOST OF THEM ARE KILLED BY HIGH TEMPERATURES.

Thus, taking the following precautions will go a long way towards preventing food poisoning:

* * **keep food cold or hot (not just warm)**
* * **keep it covered**
* * **use it within any recommended period**
* * **cook it thoroughly.**

These simple but important measures will also help slow down the inevitable process of deterioration so that the food will keep longer.

MAIN RISK

The greatest risk of food poisoning occurs when cooked food is cross-contaminated with the bacteria naturally occurring on raw meat and poultry.

For this reason utensils that have come into contact with raw meat and poultry should always be well washed before using for other purposes. Hands should also be washed between handling raw and cooked foods.

AREAS OF RISK INCLUDE

* * **Cross-contamination between raw and cooked food**
* * **Insufficient thawing of frozen poultry**
* * **Undercooking food especially meat and poultry**
* * **Cooling cooked food too slowly before refrigeration**
* * **Preparing food too far in advance**
* * **Storing food in a warm place**
* * **Not reheating food to a high enough temperature to kill food poisoning bacteria and destroy toxins**

FOOD POISONING—THE SYMPTOMS

Food poisoning symptoms can include vomiting, stomach cramps, diarrhoea, headache, fever and aching limbs.

The ill-effects of some forms of food poisoning can be felt within a few hours of eating. This is when the bacteria have formed toxins in the food itself.

With salmonella poisoning, the bacteria continue to multiply within the body and the effects may not be felt for 12-36 hours.

Whatever the cause, however, the greater the number of bacteria that are present in the food, the more rapid will be the onset and the more severe may be the symptoms.

WHAT TO DO IF IN DOUBT

Should you or someone in your family have these symptoms severely or persistently, it is always advisable to contact your doctor. Where babies and elderly people are concerned ALWAYS consult a doctor.

from Juliet Gray, *Common Sense About Food in the Kitchen*, Food & Drink Federation

Once the information was in a usable form, they began to think about introductory sentences for each section.

'In Great Britain 36% of food poisoning is caused by poultry.'

'One way food poisoning bacteria are spread is . . .'

'Food poisoning symptoms are . . .'

When his assignment was complete, it was clear and to the point. His tutor pointed out that he could use these for future assignments and these could be used for his **Wordpower** portfolio.

In future assignments, **Ansell's** work covered:

Stage 2 Unit 013 Element 1
Select material from a variety of given textual sources for a specific purpose

Stage 2 Unit 013 Element 2
Extract information from materials in textual and graphical forms for a specific purpose

Stage 2 Unit 014 Element 1
Consult a reference system to find materials for a particular purpose

Stage 2 Unit 015 Element 3
Convey information and opinions in written form.

Points to notice

1. An important element in the arrangements for **Ansell's** learning support was the liaison between the Catering Department and the basic skills tutor. The catering lecturer was able to supply background information and course handouts so that the tutor could focus the learning support sessions on relevant material and tackle topics in the right order.

2. **Ansell** was pleased that he did not have to join a class but could work on an individual learning programme. While the tutor started him off with one-to-one help, the resources in the Learning Support Workshop were organised for ease of access, and quite soon **Ansell** was able to do some of his work independently, following instructions from his Learning Plan and finding the required materials for himself.

This released the tutor to work with other students and cut out the frustrations of waiting for one overworked tutor!

Work which could be developed for an individual or a group

Gapped handouts

A cloze passage, like the reading assessment mentioned earlier, tends to have a regular pattern of omissions (e.g. every fifth word). The idea of 'filling the gaps' can be used in another way if the words missed out are selected by the tutor and represent key terms.

The student may be asked to supply the answers from memory or the answer words may be presented and the student required to make the right selection.

Form filling

Ansell asked for help in filling in an accident form (see opposite) when he had cut his finger while on placement. His tutor explained that BLOCK CAPITALS and printing were probably the clearest handwriting on this sort of form, except for the signature which would need to be in **Ansell's** usual joined up script. Because there were only a few lines of space available to explain how the accident had happened, she discussed with him which facts were important and which could be left out.

She then collected other forms which he might have to fill in the course of his work: sickness forms; insurance claims; applications for leave and travel claim forms.

After working with his tutor on filling in the accident form and doing some further practice, **Ansell** achieved Wordpower Stage 2 Unit 015 Element 1 by showing his competence in completing forms.

Form filling can be broken down into stages, and discussion should determine what is needed. Practice forms are easily made, or you can usually get some free. A number of practice books for form filling have also been published.

There are some common features which are worth pointing out.

- Forms use various phrases like **capital letters, block letters,** or **print,** which means the same.

- The section for **Name** is often broken down for example: **Surname; First names; Forenames; Christian names**; written in full.

- Your title can he presented in different forms, for example:

Mr		☐ Mr	
Mrs	CROSS OUT	☐ Mrs	TICK BOX
Miss		☐ Miss	
Ms		☐ Ms	

68

ACCIDENT FORM

1. About the person who had the accident

- Give full name
- Give the home address
- Give the occupation

Name ANSELL LAWRENCE

Address 15 BLUEBELL WALK

ANYTOWN

Postcode A24 7B

Occupation CATERING TRAINEE

2. About you, the person filling in this book

- Please sign the book and date it.
- If you did not have the accident, write your address and occupation.

Your signature   Date

A Laurence   As No. 1

Accident   As No. 1

Postcode

Occupation

3. About the accident

- Where it happened?
- When it happened?

Date   Time

5/10/97   4.15pm

In what room or place did the accident happen?

KITCHEN

Reporting of Injuries, Diseases and Dangerous Occurrences, RIDDOR 1985

For the employer only

Please initial the box provided if the accident is reportable under RIDDOR

Employer's initials   T.W.

4. About the accident – what happened?

- Say how the accident happened. Give the cause if you can.
- If any person was injured say what it is.

How did the accident happen?   I WAS CUTTING UP ONIONS IN THE KITCHEN OF THE STAR HOTEL WHERE I AM ON PLACEMENT. THE FIRE A_ARM WENT OFF, CAUSING ME TO JUMP AND CUT THE INDEX FINGER OF MY LEFT HAND. AT THE ASSEMBLY POINT I REPORTED THE ACCIDENT TO THE COOK. SHE SENT ME TO THE FIRST AID ROOM FOR A DRESSING. THIS WAS AT 4.30PM.

- Your address may need to be set out in a certain way, for example:

Road _____

Town/City _____

County _____

Postcode _____

- Your signature is different from writing out your name or printing, and you need to decide on, and stick to, a signature.
- The date can be written, for example, 17th February 1997, or in numbers 17.2 .97. Sometimes it is presented in boxes.

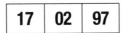

This also applies to date of birth – which often appears on forms as **d.o.b.**.

Often students will want to work on specific forms and it's useful to break each form into a number of manageable steps, and work on each in turn. Practice will probably be needed in fitting the information into the limited space available on most forms.

5 | Teaching the Skills of Literacy

> **Reading – Writing – Word level work – Sentence level – Grammar – Punctuation – Text level work – The place of oral work**

Literacy combines the important skills of reading and writing. Speaking and listening are integral skills, and work in these areas will enhance the learner's understanding and use of language in both their oral and written work.

Reading

Successful readers use a range of strategies to get at the meaning of a text. They focus on all of the elements or detail at word level, and on the text as a whole. Effortlessly shifting their focus between the two.

As reading develops, adults will depend less on the 'encoding' elements of phonics and individual word recognition, and more on the use of context and on the knowledge and experience of text.

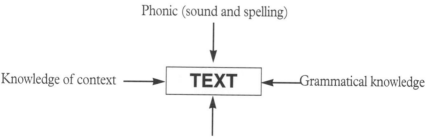

Phonic (sound and spelling)

Knowledge of context ⟶ **TEXT** ⟵ Grammatical knowledge

Word recognition and graphic knowledge

Word level strategies are important and need to be taught effectively. Beginner readers tend to see words as images with particular shapes and patterns. Tutors can encourage learners to focus in more detail on the decoding of words. This is essential when working on spelling, and it can help to build confidence for approaching unfamiliar texts.

At the sentence and text levels of reading, a wider range of strategies are taught. The learner will need to develop extended reading skills for extracting information, and analysing a text.

Writing

Writing partners and reinforces reading. The focus on word, sentence and text is equally important here. A detailed look at word and sentence level will help to focus on the organisation and accuracy of the writing. Shifting the emphasis to text will develop the extended writing skills necessary to create a wider variety of texts for a range of purposes.

This analysis reflects *The National Literacy Strategy: Framework for teaching (1998)* which gives specific guidance on which skills should be taught to children at which stages in their school life. Working with adults, similar principles can be applied. In the following sections we show how some of the word, sentence and text teaching strategies can be used, with reference to the case studies already discussed.

What is likely to differ is work with adults is:

- what they already know and the advantages and problems this will bring;
- different material;
- different pressures to learn, often to work with children.

Word level work

Word level work is concerned with phonics, spelling and vocabulary. This is particularly relevant to the beginner reader and writer – at this level, the tutor is providing the learner with useful techniques for decoding words and developing spelling strategies. This will involve work on phonics, initial sounds and consonant blends, an awareness of prefix and suffix and word families. Learners will be encouraged to notice word shapes (working in upper and lower case) to chunk words, find words within words and use memory devices to help with spelling. You can refer to the section on *Improving spelling* in the *Practical Approaches* chapter for more detail on how to develop these strategies.

 (e.g. looking at word shapes)

All of these methods were important in the work with **Norma**. As a rather unconfident beginner, this concentration on some of the detail of the text enabled her to feel she was gaining control and making progress. Her creation of a written piece using the language experience approach provided ample material to begin work at this level. Her tutor went on to devise word searches and crosswords – excellent practice in whole word recognition. **Norma** compiled a personal dictionary and also her 'survival kit' with her tutor's help. The choice of key words, social sight words and the information for easy reference in this pack was made after careful consideration. All of these strategies focused heavily on work at word level although **Norma** was also encouraged to incorporate sentence level strategies and to progress through to a focus on whole text.

Sentence level

Sentence level work is concerned with grammar and punctuation. When an adult comes along to improve basic reading skills, it is important to introduce them to sentence level work early in their programme. This emphasises from the start that words should make some sense.

Focused and progressive work at sentence level can help to make explicit the rules and conventions which the learner encounters in his reading and ultimately wants to be able to produce in his writing. To teach these structures, the tutor needs a clear overview of the grammar system

Grammar

Any English sentence is shaped by various rules and conventions. It starts with a capital letter and ends with a full stop. By gradually introducing a range of styles of reading matter and discussing and explaining the variations, tutors can support adult learners in becoming familiar with structures of expression and verbal acrobatics that they have not had access to before. That familiarity is the first step in learning to manipulate and use such structures in their own writing.

The order of words in a sentence often follows a common order, for example:

My brother	*lost*	*his hat.*
(the person or thing we are talking about)	(what he or it did)	(the thing or person affected by what he did)
The car	*failed*	*its MOT.*
The two children	*licked*	*their ice-creams.*

The benefit of these common patterns is that, as experience grows, even basic readers know what to expect. They can begin to anticipate what comes next even before looking at the word or phrase. Prediction is a skill and strategy to be encouraged.

For example, if a student correctly reads the phrase,

> *'Tony sold his –'*

and is asked to predict what the next word is, he may suggest

> – *'car', 'hose',* perhaps even *'story'.*

However, we would be totally thrown by a suggestion such as,

> – *'happened'* or *'if'* or *'clever'.*

None of these would complete the sentence in a way that made any grammatical sense. 'Why are you guessing <u>that</u> word?' we would ask. 'What does it mean?'

Managing to predict a sensible word to insert is a good measure of reading skills. This approach was taken by **Ansell's** tutor in the last chapter.

As children or adults learn to listen and speak in English, and then to read and write it, certain grammatical patterns become familiar and begin to sound right, while an uncommon juxtaposition of words sounds strange or wrong. For instance, someone may puzzle over the sentence, 'That story Tony sold.' as the word order is uncommon. Part of progress with reading is to be able to deal with less standard word order and still pull the meaning out. The order may be varied for dramatic effect, to create a more formal tone, and so on.

Some aspects of sentence construction are influenced by the purpose of the writing: who is intended to read it? what kind of writing is it? For example, the instructions on a tube of adhesive are likely to sound like 'orders'.

> *Ensure surfaces to be glued are clean and dry.*
>
> *Spread adhesive thinly on both surfaces.*
>
> *Leave for 8-10 minutes until tacky.*
>
> *Align surfaces and press firmly together for 30 seconds.*
>
> *Leave to harden for 2 hours before use.*

The imperative form is suited to providing directions that are clear and concise. We would be surprised if the writing style on the tube was different.

> *. . . I always leave it for 8 minutes or so.*
>
> *If you touch it, it should feel a bit tacky.*
>
> *Then you need to get the two bits lined up and shove them together really hard.*

We must not overlook the fact that everyone needs access to the skills of reading and writing in standard English. For many adults standard English grammar is not part of their first learned language. Sometimes the reader trying to understand a formal piece of writing may feel (like **Joe** did when reading his insurance company's letters) that the language seems designed to confuse. Local variations and differences of class, race and culture cause widely diverging experiences of spoken English. Part of the learning as people move towards fluent reading of more formal texts is to recognise and reproduce the 'other' language.

Punctuation

As we noted, a sentence starts with a capital letter and ends with a full stop. Why this is so and what else punctuation can do may often seem like a minefield to the learner. Punctuation marks are intended to be useful signals to guide the reader. They mark boundaries in the text showing which parts go together and where new points begin. As people extend their writing they need to develop the ability to use punctuation to guide the reader through the structure of the piece. Patricia's work on this is mentioned in *Part 4*.

Text level work

Text level work is concerned with the comprehension and composition of fictional and non-fictional text. Whilst the focused teaching of 'word' and 'sentence' level skills contributes to the organisation and accuracy of students' writing the context of their reading, i.e. the texts, gives structures, themes and purposes for much of their writing.

As the students' range of reading and writing increases so does their need to understand a wider variety of texts, their organisations and purposes. At the same time the tutor needs to develop teaching techniques and activities which emphasise advanced reading and composition skills at 'text' level.

It is important that reading and writing objectives are closely linked to the text students are reading i.e. those which are of interest or are particularly relevant to them at the time, in order to provide a structure for their writing. Professional emphasis needs to be placed on the skills of planning, drafting, revising, proof reading and the presentation of writing.

Much of the work done with **Joe** was to develop his text level skills. He needed to develop:

- comprehension skills to improve his understanding of the meaning and message of passages of text (minutes of union meetings) and to be able to distinguish between fact and opinion (personal correspondence).

Patricia was keen to gain qualifications and eventually pass a GCSE. Her tutor devised activities to develop **Patricia's** text level skills. She needed to develop:

- composition skills to extend her ability to write longer texts, plan, draft and edit in a variety of styles and a variety of formats (writing childhood memories).

Text and composition tasks should be sufficiently within the range of the student's current skills, understanding and experience to allow an element of success while at the same time providing scope for the development of their reading and writing skills.

The place of oral work

Oral work provides students with the opportunity to develop their speaking and listening skills which in turn enhances their understanding of language in both oral and written forms and of the way in which language is used to communicate. It is also an important part of the process through which students read and compose texts. **Joe's** tutor used oral work with him to recount the content of the union meetings he had attended and to compare it with the written minutes in order to develop his understanding of the text. The tutor could have extended this activity to develop **Joe's** awareness of the difference between spoken and written language.

Successful readers use a range of strategies to get to the meaning of a text and tutors need to ensure that text and composition tasks are sufficiently within the range of the students' current skills, understanding and experience, while at the same time providing scope for the development of their reading and writing skills.

The good tutor recognises the need to develop all three skills levels and the right time to introduce a different level. To do this the tutor has to know what skills the student has on each level and the skills to develop.

6 | Accreditation and Progression

Accreditation – Relating activities to competencies – Progress and progression – Seeking support

This chapter examines the range of ways in which students can gain recognition of their progress and discusses the competence-based approach. It looks at progression and what this may include.

Accreditation

Accreditation means gaining some sort of official recognition in the form of a record or certificate for the work one has done.

Not all basic skills students want this sort of recognition. For many, their newly acquired skills and growing confidence are reward enough. For others, basic skills tuition represents a chance for them to gain a qualification for the first time in their lives. Whether a student goes for a qualification will depend on many things such as their ambition, confidence, the time available for study and, in some cases, available finance.

For many years basic skills students had no access to any form of national accreditation. At that time, success in the school system was based on passing examinations. Because many basic level students had failed in this system, tutors understandably were not anxious to subject them to a situation that had already undermined their confidence.

In fact, in many cases the system had failed the students. Some people like **Patricia**, who went to a special school because of her disability, had never had the chance to sit examinations.

Gradually fairer methods of judging progress have been introduced. Continuous assessment, profiling and skills tests are but a few. In some areas a federation of local Open Colleges, the Open College Network, credits specific courses which are written to local needs. **Norma** could get Open College credits for the 'process work' or skills development work which she did such as punctuation, spelling and re-drafting.

However, most nationally recognised examination boards now have certificates which accredit what is now called 'basic' or 'communication skills' rather than 'literacy'. These are sometimes full qualifications in themselves or modules within wider forms of accreditation.

Many of these qualifications now come under the heading 'Entry Level' qualifications. This identifies them as stepping stones to the first level of nationally recognised qualifications.

Relating activities to competencies

In the past a criticism often made was that many basic skills certificates were little more than an attendance record. It is now accepted that most people like to know how effective their skills are, set against external criteria. It is also recognised that working on a skill does not always mean a student can use that skill in a real life situation.

There are two nationally recognised certificates called the **Certificate in Communication Skills (Wordpower)**, City and Guilds 3793 and the **Certificate in Numeracy Skills (Numberpower)**, City and Guilds 3794. They accredit a person's competency or effectiveness measured against these standards. In the Certificate in Communication Skills there are four levels of attainment:

- Entry Level
- Level 1
- Level 2
- Level 3.

Detailed guidelines called performance criteria outline exactly what a candidate must do to achieve 'competence', that is the ability to consistently achieve success in a given task. The assessment is independent of any set course or learning programme.

Students can demonstrate their effectiveness in any context they choose and if necessary can repeal the assessment a number of times until the required standard has been achieved. Evidence of successful assessment is collected into a folder which is called a 'portfolio'. This contains samples, observations and records of a candidate's assessment activities.

Tutors and students have found that the reading and writing work they have done can also be used as evidence of competence for the Wordpower certificate. For example, a letter to the Electricity Board, to complain about the size of a bill can be added to the portfolio for Wordpower. The advantage of the competence-based approach is that it allows any literacy work to be accredited and, to go towards a qualification. In this way, a student who has been working for three months on reading and writing skills can decide to go for a qualification - and will already have some work that can go into the portfolio.

Ansell was able to get evidence towards a Communication Skills Certificate using the notes and charts he needed for his catering course. Forms he filled in and assignments he wrote could be used. All this evidence, however, has to be judged against the set standards.

For instance, in finding and choosing information for his project 'Christmas Catering: the dangers' **Ansell** would be judged against the performance criteria of *Unit*

An example of a record sheet for **Ansell's** Wordpower portfolio

Unit 307

Record Sheet
Unit 307 Read and respond to textual and graphical material

Element 1
Select and use information from textual and graphical sources

Evidence indicators – your portfolio must contain:

Four occasions dealing with different contexts, at least two should combine textual and graphical presentation.

Notes on type and location of evidence		*Code*
3 Dec 97	Preparation work for 'Christmas Catering: the dangers'	CCI
7 Jan 98	Health and Safety Information on Lifting and Carrying	HS2
25 Mar 98	Information from companies for project on 'Wine'	WP1
6 April 98	Job Search Information	JS2

Performance criteria – you must be able to:

a) Identify relevant sources

b) Identify main points accurately from the textual and graphical sources

c) Identify the meaning of unfamiliar words, phrases and images accurately, using the sources provided

d) Use the information for the purpose

Range dimension and categories

Topic/context
routine non-vocational sources (e.g. newspapers, magazines, journals, child care manuals, cookery books, holiday brochures, simple textbooks and instruction manuals) routine vocational sources (e.g. letters, record cards, reports, log-book entries)

Format
textual and images/graphical sources which are in common use/circulation or from a specialism known to the reader

Images
used commonly in the context (e.g. sketches, diagrams, still photographs, charts)

Clarification of meaning
written sources provided for the individual: (e.g. dictionaries, manuals); oral sources (e.g. supervisors, tutors, colleagues). Written sources which include some graphical content, (e.g. captioned photographs, diagrams, sketches and charts).

Signatures to confirm completion (with date)

Candidate			Internal verifier	
A. Lawrence			A. J. Verifier	
Date	8th April 1998		Date	23rd April 1998

Assessor		
A. Trainer		
Date	8th April 1998	

79

307 Element 1 – Select information from textual and graphical sources. This in turn would link with the standards required in his vocational qualification in catering.

Many people have an uneven spread of basic skills. As a local shop steward **Joe** had good oral communication skills even though he had difficulties expressing himself in writing. Using what is called accreditation of prior learning or achievement (APL or APA) he could now have these skills recognised towards a certificate in Communication Skills. In his union negotiations **Joe** would often have to talk to groups of people or put a case to his management about working conditions, etc. Provided he fulfilled the required performance criteria outlining how this should be done effectively, he could achieve the unit, *Exchanging information and opinions.*

These standards have been mapped against the National Curriculum used in schools and the key skills of the accreditation system used in the workplace, the National Vocational Qualifications (NVQs). They will also link with General National Vocational Qualifications (GNVQs). Thus students will know exactly where they are and how to plan for progress.

For information on how to find out more about different qualifications see the addresses in the *Resources List* in *Part 8.*

Progress and progression

Progress means moving forward, improving skills and increasing knowledge.

Most students attend a basic skills class or group with a personal goal in mind. **Norma** went to the class at her local library for practical help after her husband died. She also received a lot of support in her bereavement. **Ansell** felt, to some extent, that he had been directed towards the Learning Support Unit but found the individual tuition helped him towards his long term career aim.

Patricia learned to use a word processor and **Joe** could discuss newspaper football reports which had previously been just too difficult.

For most students progression means moving on to a new challenge. Because of the welcoming environment of most basic skills groups for a few students they become a safe haven. They stay far too long. This has been called the "warm bath syndrome". Tutors need to accept that long term students may be a sign of the group's failure rather than its success. It is the tutor's responsibility together with the student to negotiate a realistic time schedule for achieving identified aims and objectives. The aim of all basic skills provision should be to give its members the skills and confidence to move on.

Tutors should provide the means to effect this progression. These include:

- helping the student to get an idea of how long they are going to attend the group;

- knowledge about other courses;

- local job availability;

- help with information gathering strategies;
- help with study skills;
- confidence to make decisions.

It took a great deal of encouragement for **Norma** to join the Oral History Group but she was so proud when she finally took the plunge.

It is not always easy to monitor this progression but methods of recording both formal and informal progress need to be built into class and group structures.

Seeking support

Basic skills tutors need not work in isolation but should develop a network of individual agencies as a source of ideas and information about possible progression routes. These should include:

- careers advisors;
- mainstream college lecturers;
- counsellors;
- training organisation managers;
- local Training Enterprise Councils (TECs).

7 | Materials and Resources

Range of materials – Use of materials – Making your own worksheets – The use of computer assisted learning packages – Using a cassette recorder – Using videos

This chapter looks at the types of material and resources available and gives guidelines in deciding what to use and how to use it. It also looks at points to consider when creating your own material.

Range of materials

There is a considerable range of material that can be used by tutors and students. These can be grouped as follows.

1. **Commercially produced basic skills material** – which is available for developing reading, writing, speaking and listening skills from the beginner to the pre-GCSE level student.

    This material falls into several broad categories.

    - **Everyday coping skills** – These are usually topic based and concentrate on the specific skills need to get by in everyday life.
    - **Beginner readers** – some of which have accompanying audio-tapes.
    - **Intermediate readers** – aimed at those who wish to extend their reading skills.
    - **Student support materials** – which provide basic skills support for students in work, college and training situations.
    - **General English usage materials** – to develop punctuation, grammar and spelling etc.

2. **Real life materials** – these are not specifically designed for teaching purposes and are readily available locally and in most instances are free, e.g. newspapers, local bus and train timetables, and community information packs. This type of material can be adapted or supported to enhance the learning situation. Many commercial organisations issue information and learning packs free or for a very small charge.

An example of commercially produced material

TO and AT

Date:

Have you read worksheet 125?

In Box 1 is a list of incomplete sentences. Can you think which preposition comes after each underlined word?

1. He was <u>astonished</u>................................	9. Maybe you're not <u>accustomed</u>........
2. You'll never get <u>used</u>.........................	10. I was <u>puzzled</u>....................................
3. He got <u>married</u>.................................	11. She strongly <u>objected</u>......................
4. There is no <u>solution</u>..........................	12. She showed little <u>reaction</u>...............
5. She <u>smiled</u>.......................................	13. He was very <u>sympathetic</u>...............
6. Let's <u>drink</u>..	14. What is your <u>attitude</u>......................
7. This book <u>belongs</u>.............................	15. You're not very <u>friendly</u>..................
8. Try not to <u>laugh</u>...............................	

Now rewrite the underlined words in the correct boxes below. Use a dictionary to help you if you really don't know, but try to trust what you think sounds right.

TO   AT

_____ to _____	to _____	to	_____ at
_____ to _____	to _____	to	_____ at
_____ to _____	to _____	to	_____ at
_____ to _____	to _____	to	_____ at

Which ones do you need to learn? Test yourself before you continue with the worksheet?

Now write complete sentences of your own, using all the words and prepositions.

e.g. _____

<u>Note:</u> If you use a verb after a preposition, it must be a gerund (that means ending in 'ing').

Example:

There are no answer sheets for your sentences since you have made them up yourself, so ask your teacher to check that you have used the prepositions correctly.

For more practice try worksheet 129.

from Erica Buckmaster's *Self Access Worksheets*, National Extension College

3. **Homemade material** – specially designed for teaching purposes by tutors to be used with particular individuals or groups.

Days of the Week

Mon.	is short for Monday.
Tues.	is short for Tuesday.
Wed.	is short for Wednesday.
Thurs.	is short for Thursday.
Fri.	is short for Friday.
Sat.	is short for Saturday.
Sun.	is short for Sunday.

The short way of writing the days of the week is often used on calendars, diaries and time tables.

This is a page from a calendar.

January

Mon		2	9	16	23	30
Tues		3	10	17	24	31
Wed		4	11	18	25	
Thurs		5	12	19	26	
Fri		6	13	20	27	
Sat		7	14	21	28	
Sun	1	8	15	22	29	

Which days of the week do these dates fall on?

1. 3rd January ....
2. 20th January ....
3. 29th January ....
4. 27th January ....
5. 11th January ....

6. 16th January...................................
7. 7th January...................................
8. 9th January...................................
9. 12th January...................................
10. 31st January ....

from the Manchester Adult Education Service

Your library service may stock books on basic skills and readers for the student to borrow. It is worthwhile visiting your local 'attraction' for information which could be used as a focus for a group visit, e.g. a theatre visit.

Use of materials

Choosing materials well, and using them flexibly and with skill, is an important part of basic skills teaching.

The importance of real life material cannot be overstressed. The challenge is to find commercially produced material, or devise your own worksheets which build on and enhance the learning process.

However, you need to adapt and structure real life material to make it into learning material as opposed to merely reference or example material. This will include:

* making 'cloze' exercises;
* asking a series of questions to check meaning;
* setting one or a number of tasks as follow up activity;
* asking the student to find similar material from other newspapers, magazines, letters that they have received, etc.

Keep the following points in mind.

a) *Learning Structure* – the objectives which the material should enable the student to achieve, the exact purpose of the learning material needs to be clear.

b) *Content Structure* – the experience/situations to be dealt with, and the relevant information to be presented.

c) *Design Structure* – how to put the material into a format which is attractive to the student, remembering that the layout of the material needs to be planned.

* Are the context and examples relevant to the needs of the student?
* Does it have self-checking material with it?
* Is the level of language and style suitable for the student?
* Is there a focus on the practical use of language?
* Is there any bias or stereotyping, cultural, sexist, or racist?
* Is the presentation and layout clear and attractive - size of print, legibility, amount on a page, illustrations?
* Do the illustrations show people from different ethnic backgrounds?
* Are there any cultural references which might cause difficulty to the student?
* Is it interesting?
* Is it only for use with a class or can it be used with individuals?

An example of homemade material using real life sources

YELLOW PAGES

Firms in the Yellow Pages are listed under what they do. A firm called ALPHA SIGNS makes all types of signs so it comes under 'S' for Sign Makers.

Each new section has a red heading like this:

◆ **Sign makers**

Write:

Fit the right headings over the adverts.

◆ **Vacuum cleaner repairs & servicing**

◆ _____

> **A & A ELECTRICAL**
>
> FAIR TRADES APPROVED
> NO CALL OUT CHARGE/24 HR SVCS
> Free Estimates & Advice – Work Fully Guaranteed
>
> **3 Partridge Avenue,
> Wythenshawe,
> Manchester,
> M23 8PJ.**　　　　　0161-**998** 2349

◆ _____

> # T.G. SHAW & SON　EST 1958
>
> HIGH CLASS INTERIOR/EXTERIOR
>
> ## PAINTING & DECORATING
>
> HOUSES – FLATS – COMMERCIAL
> ANY WORK – ANY AREA
> GUARANTEED WORK
> **8 MAULDETH RD, MANCHESTER M20 9ND**
>
> # 0161-445 9493

◆ **Sign makers**

> # alpha signs
>
> Specialists in
> ## PERSPEX SIGNS
> Make, Erect & Maintain
> ALL TYPES OF SIGNS
> # 0151-709 3466
> ENQUIRIES WELCOME FROM
> ALL OVER THE NORTH WEST
> Riverfront Offices. South Ferry Island
> Liverpool 3 4AJ.

◆ **Burglar alarms & security systems**

◆ **Painters & decorators**

◆ **Funeral directors**

◆ _____

> ## Chubb Alarms Limited
>
> Park 17, Moss Lane,
> Whitefield, Manchester M25 7ET
>
> **SUPPLIERS & INSTALLERS OF
> INTRUDER ALARMS · FIRE ALARMS
> C.C.T.V. SYSTEMS · ACCESS CONTROL
> MANNED GUARDING SERVICES**
>
> BSIA AND NSCIA
> APPROVED
> BS5750 REGISTERED
> FIRM　　TEL: 0161-766 8511 MANCHESTER

◆ _____

> **PEACOCKS FUNERAL SERVICE**
>
> PERSONAL ATTENTION
> PRIVATE CHAPEL OF REST
>
> Day & Night Service
>
> **736/740 Wilmslow Road,
> Disbury.**　　　0161-445 3397

- Can it be used by a student working independently?
- Can it be adapted to suit a particular student?

Making your own worksheets

There are a considerable range of resources which may be used to produce your own materials for the student. The following are some points that will help you in making worksheets. Often tutors decide to share their own materials and set up "banks of worksheets". Sharing resources can save time in lesson planning.

Points to consider

- When you make worksheets for a student make sure that you are clear about the purpose of the worksheet. Is it to introduce a new skill or topic? Is it for revision or practice? Is it for information?
- What exactly is the language skill, or function or grammatical structure that you want the student to practise?
- What skills or knowledge does the student need in order to do the worksheet?
- Check that the instructions are clear – sometimes the instructions can be more difficult than the content of the worksheet.
- Use illustrations, maps or diagrams which will give clues to the meaning of the text.
- Write clearly and space the text well. Line break if this will be helpful.
- Can you find what you are looking for in existing material – (you might save valuable time).

The Basic Skills Agency publication *An Introduction to Teaching English as an Additional Language to Adults* will help in making worksheets for an EAL student.

When using material it is important to:

- be deliberate – choose the material that will be most effective;
- take charge – you control the material rather than the other way round;
- evaluate how effective it actually was.

The use of computer assisted learning packages

The use of computers in the delivery of basic skills has been accepted for some time. Open Learning has highlighted the value of Information Communication Technology (ICT) to assist students in the acquisition of their learning objectives and has done much to enhance the development of basic skills multi-media materials.

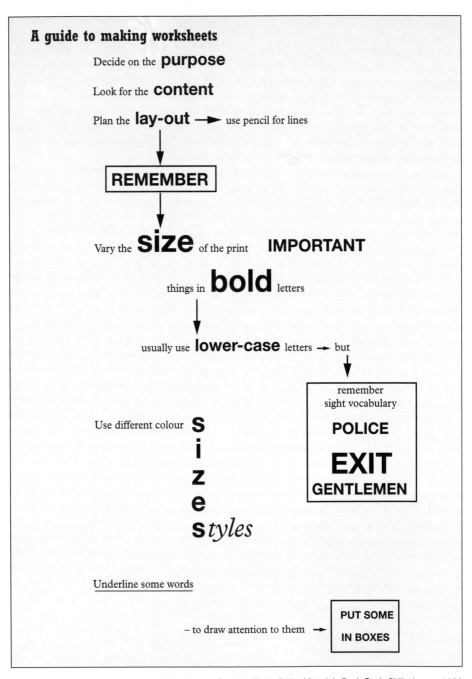

A guide to making worksheets

Decide on the **purpose**

Look for the **content**

Plan the **lay-out** ➤ use pencil for lines

↓

REMEMBER

↓

Vary the **size** of the print   **IMPORTANT**

things in **bold** letters

↓

usually use **lower-case** letters ➤ but

↓

remember
sight vocabulary

POLICE

EXIT

GENTLEMEN

Use different colour

s
i
z
e
s*tyles*

Underline some words

– to draw attention to them ➤

PUT SOME

IN BOXES

from *Initial Certificate in Teaching Basic Skills: Materials Pack*, Basic Skills Agency 1989

Computers can be used to run word processing packages which are particularly effective writing tools. Students whose written output would normally be considered poor can produce good quality copy via the word processor. Software is also available to create CVs, learn how to use the keyboard and gain other basic IT skills. These are generally described as content free software and are designed to allow the user to work on a topic at a level of their own choosing.

Some additional advantages of using content free software to develop basic skills are:

- the program can be used by students of different levels of ability;
- the user is in control of the program;
- the program is never exhausted – the options are unlimited;
- the student can acquire real computing skills whilst developing other skills.

The disadvantage for the tutor of using content free software is the need to provide support materials, however, once the materials have been developed they can be used again and again, and adapted easily to meet individual needs.

In addition to content free software, programs on CD-Rom are available to help students develop reading skills and practise writing, spelling and punctuation. These types of program are usually expensive but provide a wide range of interactive activities using videoclips and sound bites to guide and stimulate the learner. Multi-media programs instruct the learner, provide practice on what has been learned, and can help to assess performance and progress through tests. They are designed in such a way that learners can follow a course of instruction at their own pace. There are plenty of practice exercises which are marked immediately and are therefore useful as a means of independent learning. Some programs, however, are almost identical to a text book on screen and much more expensive, it is therefore wise to seek a demonstration before you decide to buy.

For further information on the use of multi-media packages and resources available see the next section.

NB – Some of the specific literacy material available has been designed for children and when choosing software it is important to make sure that the content and presentation are appropriate for adult students.

The use of ICT is developing rapidly. The University for Industry begins in the year 2000, and will use new technologies to bring education to all. The Basic Skills Agency is, for example, producing programmes that students will in future be able to watch on digital TV. The World Wide Web will also provide new ways to learn.

Using a cassette recorder

Taping Books enables the student to follow a text and gain pleasure from the story. **Norma's** tutor tapes 'Queen's Street' (Gatehouse Publications), and **Norma** eventually joined her local library and borrowed from the 'Taped Books' section. She found this to be a new recreational activity and a welcome change from watching television for stories and drama.

Sometimes, a student is hesitant when it comes to writing but still wants to 'have a go' and not to have to rely on someone else to act as a 'scribe'. Tape recorders can be very useful here. It gives the student a chance to record ideas and thoughts without having to pause and concentrate on the writing and spelling. This can be done at leisure whilst playing back the tape.

It is common for people to be a little nervous about speaking into a tape, but a bit of practice, some privacy and the use of headphones when playing back will all help to ease the problems.

Using videos

There are relatively few commercially produced videos which are available for literacy work with adults. Probably the largest resource available to basic skills staff are the programmes produced by the BBC over many years. The popular series *Spelling It Out* continues to be used by many centres. Some of the material from the *Step Up to Wordpower* is useful.

Two videos have been produced that have been distributed widely, *Spell Well at Any Age* and *Punctuate Well at Any Age and Write a Perfect Letter* (available from the Basic Skills Agency). They are designed to be followed by adults independently. It is quite possible, however, to use parts of them to illustrate particular points that you are covering in a session, e.g. the silent '*e*' rule, how to begin or end a letter, etc.

It is important to use videos in teaching as a tool for a specific purpose rather than as a blunt instrument. It is often very boring for a student or group of students to have to sit and watch a half-hour programme, just to pick up one particular teaching point. It is far better for the tutor to preview the programme and choose a short extract. Most videos will be of greatest value if accompanied by follow-up material which takes account of the needs of the group or individual student.

A bank of blank videos is useful for recording television programmes.

8 0 | Some Useful Materials and Further Reading

The Basic Skills Agency has published *Resources: a guide to basic skills material for schools and colleges (1996)* which lists a range of literacy and numeracy material. Each title has been reviewed by tutors working in basic skills.

The list below is not a comprehensive list of resources. It is simply a list of materials and contacts you might find useful. A local centre may have more books and equipment and it would be worth contacting them.

The Basic Skills Agency Resource Centre in the Institute of Education Library has a display collection of teaching materials you can visit. The Centre can answer enquiries by post, phone, fax or email.

> **Basic Skills Resource Centre, The Newsam Library,**
> **Institute of Education, 20 Bedford Way, London WC1H OAL.**
> **Tel: 0171 612 6069, Fax: 0171 612 6093, Email: lib.enquiries@ioe.ac.uk**
> **Website: http://www.ioe.ac.uk/library/bsa/**

Some publishers specialising in basic skills materials (write or ring for catalogues)

> NB – Easier reading books are more likely to be available from publishers marked with an asterisk (*).

*The Basic Skills Agency, ADMAIL 524, London WC1A 1BR. Tel: 0870 600 2400 Fax: 0870 600 2401 Website: http://www.basic-skills.co.uk

*Avanti Books (agents for many basic skills publishers), 8 Parsons Green, Boulton Road, Stevenage SG1 4QG Tel: 01438 350155 or 745876/877 Fax: 01438 741131 Email: AVANTIHIL@aol.com Website: http://members.aol.com/avantihil

British Dyslexia Association, 98 London Rd, Reading RG1 5AU

*Brown & Brown, Keeper's Cottage, Westward, Wigton, Cumbria CA7 8NQ. Tel & Fax: 01697 342915

The Chalkface Project, PO BOX 1, Milton Keynes MK5 6JB Tel: 01908 340 340 Fax: 01908 340 341 (content of some packs useful for adult students)

*Gatehouse Books, Hulme Adult Education Centre, Stretford Road, Manchester M15 5FQ Tel: 0161226 7152

*Hodder & Stoughton Educational, c/o Bookpoint Ltd, Direct Services, 78 Milton Park, Abingdon, Oxon OX14 4TD Tel: 01235 400405 Fax: 01235 400454 Email: orders@bookpoint.co.uk

*LDA (Learning Development Aids), Duke Street, Wisbech, Cambridgeshire PE13 2AE (mainly primary curriculum, but some useful teenage/young adult reading series) Tel: 01945 463441 Fax: 01945 587361

London Language & Literacy Unit, Southwark College, Southampton Way, London SE5 7EW Tel: 0171 639 9512 Fax: 0171708 4751

MCH Publications, PO BOX 3720, Redditch, Worcestershire B97 5EF Tel: 01386 792755/870825

National Extension College, 18 Brooklands Avenue, Cambridge CB2 2HN Tel: 01223 316644 Fax: 01223 313586 Email: nec@dial.pipex.com Website: http://www.nec.ac.uk

Scottish Community Education Council, Rosebery House, 9 Haymarket Terrace, Edinburgh EH12 5EZ Tel: 0131313 2488 Fax: 0131313 6800 Email: SCEC@scec.dircon.co.uk   Website: http://www.qedi.co.uk

Stanley Thornes, Ellenborough House, Wellington Street, Cheltenham, Gloucestershire GL50 14D Tel: 01242 228888 Fax: 01242 253695

Start reading

Basic Skills Work Cards (gardening, DIY etc), PRU (from Avanti)

Ben Books (various simple readers), BEN (from Avanti)

Brown & Brown (e.g. *The Accident* series of minibooks & exercises), Brown & Brown

A Day in the Life Series (7 readers – one for each day), PRU (from Avanti Books)

Day to Day Readers (12 'soap' readers based around a community), Basic Skills Agency

Gatehouse Books (easy readers, most with cassettes)

Hats (short stories about women's lives), Basic Skills Agency

Natal University New Readers Project Books (from Avanti)

New Zealand Readers, Porinua Language Project (from Avanti)

Pam and Tom Reading Scheme (a structured reading scheme with worksheets) (from Avanti)

P.A.T. (Phonological Awareness Training): a new approach to phonics, Buckinghamshire Educational Psychology Service (Tel: 01296 394462) (a structured scheme for children that could help new adult readers with reading fluency and spelling)

Spike Readers, Spike Press (from Avanti)

ViVa Readers (attractive, South African series, some with only one line of text per page), ViVa Books (from Avanti)

Widening and developing reading

Five Minute Thrillers (a series of tiny books, each with its own tape), LDA

Friends, Families & Folk Tales (students' writing with activities for English development), London Language & Literacy Unit

The Graphic Shakespeare Series, Evans Brothers

Livewire – Real Lives, Chillers, Youth Fiction & Plays (includes biographies from the world of sport, film, history, politics & music), Hodder & Stoughton

News Worksheets (published 3 times a year), Brown & Brown

Penguin Readers (or similar graded, simplified books such as the *Oxford Bookworms* series – pick authors according to the interests of the students)

Still Standing in the Plant Pot (& other poetry books), Spike Press (from Avanti)

Real Lives – Bollywood Series (5 biographies of Asian film stars), Basic Skills Agency

A Stab in the Heart, Basic Skills Agency

Spirals (readers & plays), Stanley Thomas

Axed Between the Ears and *Earshot*, both by David Kitchen, Heinemann (poetry anthologies – accessible and popular with students)

Newspapers, magazines, publicity and information leaflets are excellent sources of reading material. Many local basic education schemes produce their own books which could be useful.

Improve your writing

These books encourage and develop writing by offering ideas, tips for functional writing, exercises and stimulus for further written work.

Finding the Words, Brown & Brown

Correspondence Rules OK and similar packs from Chalkface Project (some Chalkface packs are not suitable for adult students)

Getting to Grips with Writing (other *Getting to Grips* titles also useful), Letts Educational

Left to Write, Brown & Brown

Opening Time, Gatehouse

Practise Your Punctuation, Tower Hamlets College (from Avanti)

Self-Access Form Filling, National Extension College

Sentences Success, MCH Publications

Writing and Punctuation Packs from Oxford ABLE (from Avanti)

Writing Letters, National Extension College

Writing Support Packs, Liverpool (COLCC) & Crosby (AEC) (from Avanti)

Self-Access, Grammar, NEC

Self-Access, Formal Letters 1, Formal Letters 2, Oxford ABLE

Self-Access, Check Your Punctuation, Books A,B,C, Oxford ABLE

Self-Access, Writing Cards, Oxford ABLE

Self-Access, Writing Short Letters and Notes, Oxford ABLE.

Self-Access, Writing Cheques, Oxford ABLE

Self-Access, Check Your Punctuation, self-assessment pack, Oxford ABLE

Spelling and dictionaries

Black's Writing Dictionary, A & C Black

The Cassell Spelling Dictionary, Cassell

Collins Plain English Dictionary, Collins

Heinemann English Dictionary, Heinemann

Longman Photo Dictionary, Longman

Spell It Yourself, Oxford

Foundation Spelling, MCH Publications

Helping Adults to Spell, Basic Skills Agency

Self-access Worksheets, National Extension College

The Spelling Pack, Basic Skills Agency

Spelling Worksheets, Brown & Brown

Unscrambling Spelling, Hodder & Stougton

Listening and talking

Introducing Key Communication, MCH Publications

Key Words: Developing and Assessing Basic Communication Skills, National Extension College

Succeeding at Interviews, National Extension College

Talking Rules OK!, Chalkface Project

Learning to learn

Developing Learning Skills, National Extension College

How to Study Effectively, National Extension College

Learning Skills Resource Bank, National Extension College

Study Skills for 16-Plus, Chalkface Project

Software

The New Reading Disc, CTAD (PC only)

Words in Action, IBM

World Power, Workforce (helps deliver Foundation Level Wordpower – PowerMac/Apple only)

The Worksheet Generator Upgrade, Basic Skills Agency (available September/October 1999)

Key Skillbuilder, NEC

Key Skills Collection, NEC

Basic Skills, Heinemann

The Jobsearch Reading Disc, CTAD and Basic Skills Agency

Learning for Work, Workbase (workbooks addressing workplace skills linked to Workbase's assessment programme)

For further information on using computers in literacy teaching, contact:

BECTA (British Educational Communications & Technology Agency), Milburn Hill Road, Science Park, Coventry CV4 7EZ Tel: 01203 416669 Fax: 01203 411418 Website: http://www.becta.org.uk/

Background information and ideas

Diagnosing Dyslexia, Basic Skills Agency

On Course (series of videos, e.g. *Working on Reading*), Basic Skills Agency

Literacy Today

Information about qualifications

Qualifications for staff

Initial Certifcate in Teaching Basic Skills (9281)
This is a pre-scrvice training programme for people who wish to teach or assist in the teaching of literacy on a 1:1 basis or in support of a more experienced member of staff.

Certificate in Teaching Basic Skills (9285) (NVQ Level 3&4)
This is a competence based profile scheme. It is suitable for staff with a minimum of 6 months experience in teaching literacy and who have undertaken initial training.

Basic Skills Support in Further Education (7324/02) and Basic Skills Support in the Workplace (324/03)

The further education certificate is aimed at lecturers and tutors in who are not basic skills specialists but need to provide support to students on vocational or academic courses. The workplace certificate is intended for trainers in the workplace who are responsible for supporting employees. Both are competence based awards and candidates generate performance evidence from teaching experience.

Further details on these courses from: City & Guilds, 1 Giltspur Street, London EClA 9DD Tel: 0171 294 2468 Fax: 0171294 2400.
Website: http://www.city-and-guilds.co.uk/

Qualifications for students

Communication Skills (Wordpower-3793), City & Guilds

Four levels are available. Assessment is by gathering evidence of the use of basic skills in everyday life and there is no examination.

For details of other qualifications contact your local college or refer to: *Accreditation in Literacy/Numeracy/ESOL and Core Skills,* published by the London Language and Literacy Unit.

AN INTRODUCTION TO

LITERACY
TEACHING

Compiled by Rose Gittins

The Working Group

The Revision Team:

Rose Gittins, Director of Client Services, MAES

Sheila Simpson, Training Services Manager, MAES

Pauline Walker, Lecturer – Professional Development/Teacher Education MAES

Moira Welch, Basic Skills/Key Skills Consultants

The 1998 revision includes contributions from the original working group.

Carole Whitehurst
Joyce Bradley
Doreen Jones
Nadine Newsome